# HAND-REARING PARROTS
## and other birds

# HAND-REARING
# PARROTS
## and other birds

*Rosemary Low*

BLANDFORD

First published in the UK 1987 by Blandford Press
A division of Cassell Publishing plc
Artillery House, Artillery Row, London SW1P 1RT

Reprinted 1988
Reprinted 1989

Distributed in the United States by
Sterling Publishing Co, Inc,
2 Park Avenue, New York, NY 10016

Distributed in Australia by
Capricorn Link (Australia) Pty Ltd
387 Park Avenue South, New York, NY 10016-8810

**British Library Cataloguing in Publication Data**

Low, Rosemary
    Hand-rearing parrots and other birds.
    1. Parental behavior in animals 2. Birds
    —Behavior
I. Title
    598.256      QL698.3

ISBN 0 7137 1901 X

Typeset by Nene Phototypesetters Ltd, Northampton
Printed in Great Britain by
Bath Press Ltd, Avon

*This book is dedicated to K. C. Lint,
Curator of Birds at San Diego Zoo in California
for 28 years until his retirement in 1976. A pioneer
of hand-rearing, his techniques are still in use today.
During 40 years at San Diego Zoo he bred more
than 500 species of birds and hand-reared
hundreds of parrots and many other
species from Hummingbirds to
Andean Condors.*

# CONTENTS

# ACKNOWLEDGEMENTS

I am indebted to Professor T. G. Taylor for his valuable comments on the dietary requirements of parrot chicks. Thanks are also due to P. J. S. Olney for permission to reproduce the table of food intake in Vulture chicks from the *International Zoo Yearbook*, to G. A. Smith for permission to reproduce his line drawing of a Caique chick, to Chris Blackwell for providing the excellent photographs of parrot chicks being hand-reared by Mr and Mrs H. T. Sissen, and to R. H. Grantham and Ulf Rohlin for their photographic contributions.

The line drawings are by Anita Lawrence.

# INTRODUCTION

Hand-rearing is one of the most rewarding and fascinating aspects of aviculture. The means of saving chicks which would die due to lack of parental care, it can be a great source of satisfaction, both as a practical method of increasing the number of young bred and for the emotional experience. The end product is often a beautiful youngster which would otherwise have been discarded as a corpse weeks or days previously.

Hand-rearing is also an important tool in the breeding of endangered species, being the most effective way of rapidly increasing the numbers of birds which would normally produce only one clutch per year. When eggs are removed for artificial incubation or chicks at an early age for hand-rearing, the result is usually that the female lays again.

However, the successful breeder of birds which are not endangered must keep a sense of proportion and should allow the female to attempt to rear her young to fledging on occasions. The removal of her eggs and chicks constitutes a considerable physiological shock, and also a severe emotional shock, not only in the larger species which are better able to communicate their feelings. This technique is being abused by some breeders who never allow pairs to rear their young and who sell all their offspring as pets.

Hand-reared birds excel in this role, but they are also of great value as breeding birds. Most remain tame or fearless all their lives, thus rarely suffer stress – the factor which makes birds susceptible to disease and which results in nervous parents, more likely to kill or maim their young when disturbed.

The number of letters received from breeders desperately seeking help on matters concerning hand-rearing increases with every passing year. Often they do not know to whom to turn, or have been offered poor advice which has resulted in the loss of chicks. 'Please write a book on hand-rearing, explaining everything', is an oft-repeated plea. I hope this book fills an important gap in the avicultural literature, assists many

*The author (right) and presenter Wincey Willis, hand-feeding chicks, on a breakfast television programme.*

breeders to achieve success and gives others the confidence to make their first attempt at hand-rearing.

Unless we use every means at our disposal to rear more and more birds the 1980s will be looked back on as the decade of lost avicultural opportunity – for many of the species with which we are familiar today will be unknown to future aviculturists unless we make the effort to establish them firmly in captivity now. . . .

# 1

# REASONS
# FOR HAND-REARING

Many breeders have no intention of hand-rearing young; they see rearing as a demanding task best left to the parents. In many circumstances this is true; nevertheless, sooner or later they find themselves with orphaned or abandoned chicks. There are then only three options. They could let them die, which is unthinkable. They might be able to foster them to the nests of other birds, whether or not of the same species (this is dependent on the chicks being approximately the same size or age as those of the other birds, and on being similar or related species or having a female which will accept chicks of totally different species). The third option is to rear by hand.

It may be that the task is forced on them and it is undertaken with great reluctance. Most breeders approach the role of foster parent with trepidation, which is understandable. More often than not, though, they soon discover that it is easier than they thought possible.

There are a number of different situations which will result in the need to hand-rear chicks of parrots hatched in cages or aviaries. The principal ones are as follows.

1) The death or illness of the parent(s). This rarely occurs.

2) Chicks which hatch during cold weather and which the parents cease to brood before they have acquired enough down or feathers to survive without being brooded. This is a very common cause of death in many species, including Cockatiels, lories, Australian parrakeets and others. Often the breeder is very puzzled to find the chicks dead because previously they were well cared for and he or she is not aware that the parents had ceased to brood them.

3) Failure to feed chicks at all (rare) or inadequate feeding (fairly common). This may be due to inexperience and in subsequent nests the

parents may rear their young successfully. On the other hand they may prove to be inadequate parents on all future occasions.

4) Serious plucking of young by one or both parents (common). If left in the nest they may be so badly denuded that they could die from chilling on leaving the nest and/or be unable to fly. It is advisable to remove the chicks well before they are due to leave the nest as the older they are the more difficult they are to feed initially.

5) To supply very tame birds as pets. This is very widely practised in the USA where many breeders remove all young parrots for hand-rearing as a matter of course. To date, in Europe, this attitude is rare and, generally speaking, parent-rearing is preferred unless there is a valid reason for hand-rearing. It should be pointed out that a young parrot removed from its parents as soon as it is independent and kept in a cage in a dwelling house will usually become tame quite soon, provided that it is constantly exposed to human company, love and attention. It is therefore not essential to hand-rear chicks if a tame bird is required. However, hand-reared birds are automatically tame and this fact appeals to those who breed parrots to supply the pet trade. Such birds command higher prices because the task of taming them is unnecessary.

The consequences of selling all hand-reared parrots as pets should be considered by those who practise this. Breeding pairs are not immortal. The wise breeder will retain one of his young birds and exchange another for an unrelated youngster to make up a second pair which will be ready to breed in a few years' time. This is most important with the rarer species, with large parrots where breeding age females are usually in short supply and with species which are not frequently bred in captivity.

Secondly, the wise breeder will sell some hand-reared youngsters for breeding purposes, making up unrelated pairs where possible. If, as happens in the USA, hand-reared parrots of the larger species are almost invariably sold as pets, there could be an acute shortage of breeding pairs in a few years' time, when importations of wild-caught parrots are drastically reduced or have ceased entirely.

The only redeeming factor in selling hand-reared birds as pets is that some pet owners eventually become breeders. When their pet matures they understand its need for a mate or they become absorbed in the quite different sphere of bird breeding rather than pet keeping. Former pets are usually excellent as breeding birds.

6) In the breeding of rare and endangered species, in order to increase the numbers in captivity as quickly as possible. When eggs or young are removed from the nest, the female usually lays again, whereas some

*Increasing the numbers of endangered species, such as these Tahiti Blue Lories (Vini peruviana), is an important reason for hand-rearing young. Those shown here are from three successive clutches of one pair, a nestling, a nine-month-old bird and one of five months still in immature plumage.*

species are normally single-brooded unless eggs or very young chicks are lost. Most parrots re-cycle (lay another clutch) within three weeks. Those which are seasonal layers (e.g. Australian parrakeets) generally lay only within a period of about five months in one year, whereas continuous layers (Eclectus Parrots, and many lories) may lay in any month and could produce as many as five or six clutches in one year when eggs or young are removed.

7) In tropical and sub-tropical climates predators and biting insects can cause the death of chicks in the nest. Snakes and ants cause serious problems in some areas, including the southern states of the USA.

8) To prevent a parent from attacking its young when they fledge. Some males habitually attack some (male?) offspring, most commonly cock-atoos, but even some individuals of small species. I know of a male Goldie's Lorikeet (usually a docile species) in which this occurs.

9) Occasionally breeders hand-rear young in order to have tame birds for breeding. This applies to such species as the Australian Pileated or Red-capped Parrakeet (*Purpureicephalus spurius*) which is particularly nervous. Better breeding results will be obtained with hand-reared birds because they are less easily stressed. They are therefore less likely to

13

break eggs, kill chicks or show any other tendencies resulting from a nervous disposition. It is difficult to persuade some parrot breeders that hand-reared birds make excellent parents; they harbour the belief that because they have not been reared naturally they will not know how to feed their young. This is totally untrue. It would be many generations before an instinct as old as the species itself was bred out of it.

Among my own birds I have had hand-reared parrots which were far better parents than their wild-caught parents. This is not exceptional. No experienced breeder is biased against using hand-reared birds for breeding purposes because he or she knows that they are as satisfactory as parent-reared birds in most cases. The occasional one which proves useless for breeding is found among all types of parrots, whether wild-caught, parent-reared or hand-reared.

10) There is another reason for hand-rearing which deserves mention. The best way for the breeder to understand the needs of a chick, and to observe its development, is to remove one or two from the nest for hand-rearing. Even years of breeding parrots and observing them in the nest does not provide the same insight and depth of understanding into chick care. It results in the breeder being better able to distinguish an ailing chick when he sees one in the nest and, having had the experience of hand-rearing, the confidence to remove one which is not being properly cared for by the parents.

Learning about hand-rearing on a common and inexpensive species is to be recommended, rather than suddenly being faced with experimenting on a chick which is valuable financially or perhaps for sentimental reasons.

When removing chicks from the nest only to gain experience, a start should be made with chicks aged about eight to ten days, never with newly-hatched young. A lory would be an ideal species with which to start; they are easy to feed and especially easy to wean.

## ALTERNATIVES TO HAND-REARING

In the emergency situations described above, are there any alternatives to removing chicks from the nest on a permanent basis in order to rear them?

### Foster Parents

Mention of foster parents has already been made. They are more likely to be used by the specialist breeder (of Cockatiels or Lovebirds, for example) who will almost certainly have chicks of a similar age in another nest. Most females quickly accept such chicks, of the same or of an allied species, but care must be taken not to overburden the foster parents. The youngest chick, whether fostered or belonging naturally, may fail to obtain its fair share of the food and will die, if there are too many chicks. A few species are known for their readiness to accept chicks of other species; the Redrump Parrakeet (*Psephotus haematonotus*) is one. Many female Redrumps will feed chicks of unrelated species and have even been known to feed two or three species in one nest. Such birds are exceptional, however.

In choosing foster parents an attempt must be made to use related species. Cockatoos can be fostered under Cockatiels but because of their behaviour and food soliciting vocalisations, cockatoo chicks are not likely to be fed by other species. Cockatiels are, in fact, members of the Cockatoo family and, as such, differ from all other parrots.

Several species of Conure, such as the Red-bellied (*Pyrrhura frontalis*), make excellent foster parents for neotropical species such as Amazons, in the first few days of their life. As soon as the chicks outgrow their foster parents they should be removed for hand-feeding.

Budgerigars can be used to foster Grass Parrakeets, but not Cockatiels. On very rare occasions I have heard of Budgerigars feeding Cockatiel chicks but generally they reject them.

## Supplementary Feeding

If no foster parents are available and hand-feeding is out of the question, or temporarily so, in some cases where the need is occasioned by poor feeding on the part of the parents, supplementary feeds can be given. If chicks seldom have full crops, helping the parents can be the answer. The first feed should be given as early in the morning as possible because this is when the chick is at its most vulnerable. If it is cold and has been unfed it could become so weak that it will not solicit for food. The parents will therefore not feed it and it will become progressively weaker and die. If, as well as being unfed, it is cold, it can be taken into the house, warmed in an incubator or brooder until it is strong enough to take food, and returned to the nest.

If small parrots are to be removed on a regular basis for supplementary feeding, it is quicker to remove the nest-box, rather than the chick from the nest. Supplementary feeding should not fill the crop to capacity as the chick should be receptive if the parents wish to feed it. It should be weighed daily (see page 57) to check on its progress.

Supplementary feeding usually has the added advantage of producing chicks which are tame and steady without the full-time care involved in total hand-feeding. However, it should not be commenced just before a youngster is due to leave the nest, as at this time it will be at its most nervous and difficult to feed.

# 2

# BROODERS

A brooder can be described simply as a heated container for chicks, and it can take many forms. It is, to me, an essential piece of equipment, for I have never hand-reared a chick without one. However, this has been done many times, when a 'temporary' emergency arrangement for providing heat has proved satisfactory. For example, chicks have been reared in boxes placed on a heated towel rail, inside an airing cupboard, on a radiator or, perhaps, under a lamp suspended over a box. In warm climates only very small chicks will require a heated environment as the heat generated by their nest mates will prove sufficient.

However, there is one important factor lacking with these methods of supplying heat. There is no control of the temperature. The chicks could become overheated or chilled. A thermostat controlling the heat source is therefore recommended. I prefer the use of two 60W light bulbs situated in the roof. With underfloor heating the chicks are too near the false floor which can become very hot and result in fatalities. The chick is further from the heat source with overhead heating and accidents are less likely to occur.

## MAKING A BROODER

A brooder is basically a box made of wood or a material which is easier to clean, such as Melamine, plastic or glass. A front or top made of glass or Perspex is preferable because one is able to see at a glance, without opening the brooder, what the chicks are doing. For this reason I dislike the use of totally enclosed brooders or containers. Chicks are more confident in human company when able to see out at all times. I have seen some kept in plastic buckets which lunged or hissed when uncovered. This is partly because they are suddenly exposed to hands reaching down from above; they do not see the approach.

If a chick is behaving abnormally, usually an indication of problems,

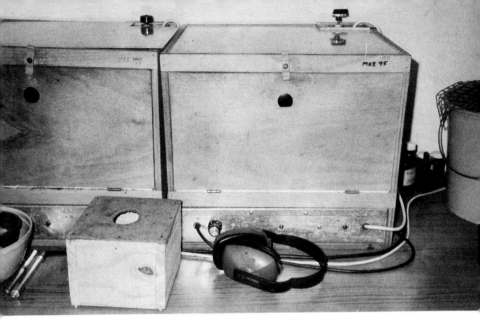

*Two glass-topped brooders, with different temperature settings for chicks of different ages, are used by H. T. Sissen. Note the ear-plugs used when feeding chicks: the chorus made by a large number can be deafening.*

this may not be noticed if it is uncovered only at feeding times. My brooders are kept in the most lived-in room in the house and as they have glass or Perspex fronts any abnormality is quickly noticed.

The situation of the brooder needs to be considered carefully – before it is constructed. Build it to fit into a convenient alcove, cupboard top, bookcase or working surface in the most occupied room. Do not place it in an outhouse because night visits may be necessary. Locate it where access is easy and it is not vulnerable to knocks by children or cats jumping on top; both might alter the thermostat setting with disastrous results. Place it near a power point or where no long trailing lead will be in evidence.

Access to the brooder can be via a hinged lid, a glass front that slides up and down or through a large door in the side. That which is most convenient for the site should be chosen.

If the heat source is in the roof, make the base of the brooder removable for ease of cleaning. If the heat is on the floor, construct a false floor above it; it can be made to slide in like a tray. The light bulbs must be inaccessible to the chicks. Lories especially are inclined to reach up and test surfaces with their tongue as they approach the feathering stage and after. They could be badly burned if the bulbs are uncovered and within reach.

The thermostat should also be placed out of harm's way. Some

*This brooder is an adapted hospital cage, with under-floor heating and a glass front which lifts up for access. The occupants are a Duivenbode's Lory (*Chalcopsitta duivenbodei*) (left) and a Tahiti Blue Lory (*Vini peruviana*).*

aquarium thermostats are suitable for the purpose and advice can be sought from an aquarists' supplier or at a large pet shop.

It must be remembered that a thermostat controls the heat by switching the bulbs off when the brooder reaches the required temperature and switching them on again when necessary. If the bulbs are placed under the floor it is necessary to have a small pilot light so that it can be seen at a glance if they are operating without pulling out the false floor. If the light is on all the time it may indicate that only one bulb is operating and the other must be replaced. The light bulbs must be checked daily in case one needs to be replaced. Failure to do so could have disastrous consequences.

There are at least two alternatives to the purpose-built brooder.

## INCUBATORS

Occasionally it is possible to buy second-hand infant incubators from hospitals. These are excellent. They are expensive but worth the outlay if large numbers of chicks are to be reared. They are ideal for very young chicks which require more careful control of the environment than older chicks.

## ADAPTING AN AQUARIUM

An even more practical alternative (infant incubators take up a lot of space) is an aquarium. It is very easy to clean and gives good views of the occupants. There are two possible methods of heating. One is a heat pad with an adjustable heat control. This is effective in warmer climates, such as the southern states of the USA. A towel should be wrapped around the pad and another towel placed over most of or part of the top of the aquarium, depending on the degree of heat required.

Alternatively, one can fit to the aquarium a roof of wood or metal which contains two light bulbs and a thermostat or dimmer.

To prevent heat loss three sides of the aquarium can be covered on the outside with polystyrene. There is no finer insulating material and polystyrene ceiling tiles are excellent for the purpose.

When using an aquarium for lory chicks of the larger species, it is advisable to make a false floor of welded mesh. Even though the bottom of the brooder is lined with several newspapers and a layer of wood chippings, after 24 hours this will be completely soaked by only two chicks. If a false floor of welded mesh is used, it is not necessary to line the bottom of the aquarium which can simply be emptied and washed daily.

*A brooder made from an aquarium, the sides of which have been insulated with polystyrene.*

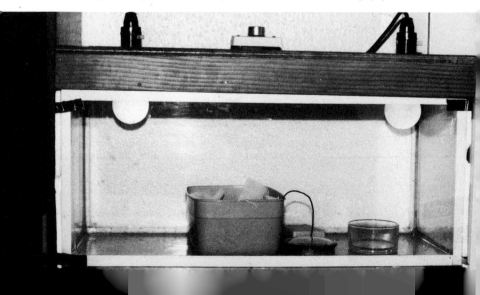

## TEMPERATURE

When heating a brooder of any description, the choice is basically between using a thermostat to control the temperature or a dimmer to achieve the required temperature. Both methods have advantages and disadvantages. With a thermostat the light is turned on when the desired temperature is reached and off before the temperature is exceeded. I employed this system for years, using red light bulbs, and chicks never appeared to suffer any discomfort from the lights switching on and off. This might occur if uncoloured bulbs were used because the glare would be too strong. The advantage of this method over the use of a dimmer is that if one bulb fails the temperature will be maintained, or nearly so, by the second bulb. Also, and this is very important, fluctuating temperatures outside the brooder will affect the temperature inside when a dimmer is used, whereas with a thermostat the temperature inside will be maintained regardless of the outside temperature. During the night the temperature in a dimmer-operated brooder could drop several degrees or – and this is perhaps even more dangerous – it could possibly overheat because it is not being opened at intervals, thus allowing cold air to enter. Maintaining the correct temperature is crucial in the case of very young chicks, thus the use of a thermostat is safer.

The standard type of dimmer used for dimming lights in a room is easily obtainable, however, and less expensive than a thermostat. The dimmer and light bulbs can be fixed to the roof of the brooder (see Fig. 1). Two 31 mm (1¼ in) holes should be made to take the sockets for the light bulbs. These are wired to the wooden roof through the dimmer

*Fig. 1   Top for aquarium brooder.*

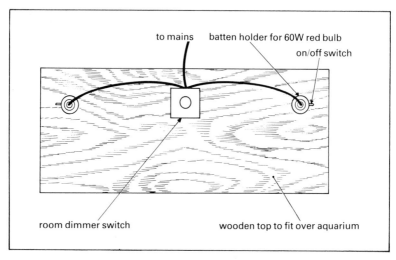

to mains   batten holder for 60W red bulb

on/off switch

room dimmer switch

wooden top to fit over aquarium

switch into a fused plug. The dimmer must also be fixed to the roof. Using a thermometer to check the temperature, the dimmer is adjusted according to the heat required. A low heat will produce a dim light only. The ideal instrument for use with a dimmer is an electronic digital thermometer. It is quite expensive but provides *instant* adjustment to the desired temperature. This is something which cannot be achieved when a thermostat is used as its reaction is slower and needs to be carefully checked.

The only disadvantage of the dimmer is that should one bulb fail the temperature will drop quickly. One breeder calculated that with two 40W bulbs 'set' with dimmer and thermometer to 29°C (85°F), the temperature dropped ten degrees in four hours when one light was switched off (Cooke, 1985). A greater heat loss would occur if one bulb failed during the early part of the night with possibly fatal consequences to very small chicks. For this reason it is preferable to use 60W or 80W bulbs.

The bulbs can be controlled by separate on/off switches. As chicks grow, one can be switched off during the day, allowing chicks to move out of the heat to the unheated end of the brooder, if they desire.

A type of heater which can be used in the brooder which gives out heat but no light is the ceramic infra-red. Unlike the type of infra-red lamp for human use, which gives out light, and which has a very limited life, the type designed for animal husbandry and horticultural use is shatter-proof and lasts indefinitely. However, chicks should be at least 20 cm (8 in) away from the lamp.

For many years I have used Salamander true infra-red lamps for sick birds. In my opinion they have no equal and are equally useful in brooders. They will not shatter even if sprayed with water when operating, they are guaranteed for 12 months, although will last for several years if handled carefully and, unlike some infra-red lamps, the emission does not affect the vitamin content of food. Manufactured by Infrared Internationale Ltd (52 St Francis Road, Salisbury, Wiltshire SP1 3Q2, England), they are made in 100W, 150W and 250W.

How does one heat a brooder if electricity is not available? A hot water bottle can be used as a temporary measure. The container in which the chicks are kept should be partly filled with sawdust or wood shavings, then placed on top of a covered hot water bottle. It would need to be refilled with hot water during the night for very small chicks. Such an arrangement can only be used on a temporary basis because a constant temperature is not obtained.

It can be used during a power cut. However, anyone regularly rearing chicks in a locality subject to frequent loss of power would be advised to install their own generator.

In one instance, a power cut caused the loss of a number of parrot chicks belonging to a friend. It resulted in the inverter cutting in. This produced only about 50 cycles per second of electricity which was insufficient and caused the electro-thermostat to burn out. In a matter of minutes the temperature rose so high that all the chicks died.

## HYGIENE

Hygiene within the brooder is very, very important. When constructing a brooder bear in mind that the best material to use is one which can be cleaned easily. I have used wood but find that a synthetic material, such as Melamine, or glass is to be preferred because it is easier to wipe clean. If wood is used ensure that the surface is smooth, and paint it. All internal surfaces should be wiped daily using a clean cloth, or paper towel which can be disposed of afterwards.

It is important that there is good circulation of air within the brooder or the glass front or the walls will be running with condensation; and, in this damp atmosphere, moulds and fungi could thrive. To assist in air circulation small holes should be made at the top and bottom of the purpose-built brooder.

In very hot climates lack of circulation of air is especially problematical. This was overcome in chicks being reared at San Antonio Zoo in Texas by mounting the incubator lid of a Marsh Farms Turn-X incubator on top of the brooder box, with the heating element turned off.

The most important item of 'furniture' within the brooder is the cardboard or plastic container used to hold the chicks. Cardboard boxes should be disposed of after two or three weeks. Plastic containers, such as ice-cream cartons, should be wiped clean or washed daily, and renewed or disinfected after each set of occupants.

Very young chicks are best placed on soft paper tissues below which is a layer of paper towel, with wood shavings on the base or several layers of paper towel. The tissue is dispensed with after the chicks are a few days old so that they are resting on paper towel.

For the first few days the surface next to the chick should be changed after each feed. Not only does this ensure that the conditions are as sanitary as possible, but it also allows one to observe the frequency of the chicks' bowel movements and the colour and condition of the faeces.

Before the chicks' eyes open the paper towel can be dispensed with and replaced by welded mesh. The size will depend on the species but ½ in square is suitable for most. It should not be so large that there is a danger of a chick's leg becoming trapped in it. After a few more days the chicks can be allowed to move freely within the brooder – not in the box – thus the brooder needs to be large enough to enable them to move about comfortably without standing in their own droppings, if they are not on wire. Some chicks void into corners at all times, and can be seen moving backwards in order to do so.

For chicks not standing on welded mesh the base of the brooder should be covered in wood chips or wood shavings. Great care must be taken in obtaining these as some purchased from wood yards could originate from treated wood and could prove harmful to chicks. The type I favour is obtainable in the UK in compressed packs under the name of Pet Litter (Petcraft brand) and is packaged by Thomas's of Halifax, England. (Do not confuse this with cat litter – gravel treated with chemicals which are harmful to birds.)

Some chicks try to pick up this litter which could be swallowed with fatal results. Such a chick should be placed on a false floor of welded mesh immediately it is seen to do so. The droppings fall through on to newspaper or sawdust placed below. The wire mesh base must be cleaned often because droppings will adhere to part of the wire. The welded mesh floor should be raised at least 2.5 cm (1 in) off the base of the brooder.

Some breeders in the USA use crushed maize as a bedding instead of wood shavings, as they have experienced the latter splintering or blocking the crop, whereas if crushed maize is ingested it causes no harm.

Whatever type of bedding is used, it must be changed frequently so that the brooder remains as dry and hygienic as possible.

# 3

# TEMPERATURE REQUIREMENTS OF CHICKS

It is often difficult for the newcomer to hand-feeding to assess the best temperature for chicks. A number of factors need to be taken into consideration, such as age, the environment from which the chick has come, species, individual requirements and the number of chicks in the brooder.

Newly-hatched parrot chicks generally require a temperature between 33.3 and 37.7° C (92 and 100° F). Incubator-hatched chicks which have come immediately from the incubator will initially require a temperature similar to that in the incubator. Within a few hours this can be decreased gradually a degree or two. Newly-hatched chicks from outdoor aviaries, or those of a few days old, may appear uncomfortable at a temperature above 33.3° C (92° F), or even above 31.6° C (89° F). If a chick is too hot it will be restless, constantly throwing itself about. In extreme cases it may be gasping.

A chick which is cold appears lethargic, and feels cold to the touch, or not warm; the food is digested slowly and this could result in sour crop (see page 60).

If the temperature is too low growth will be slower than normal and the chick's resistance to disease will be lowered.

Several young chicks together are good temperature indicators. If it is too hot they will separate to the corners of the container (normally they would be touching). Small chicks can die in a few minutes if overheated; this is why thermostatic control is so important. A chick which is too cold would survive for some hours; if not subjected to a low temperature for too long most can be revived quickly using an infra-red lamp or by placing them in a brooder or incubator, wrapped in a soft paper tissue. This has often been successful with chicks from outside aviaries which the parents have ceased to brood.

It should be remembered that newly-hatched chicks of small species are more likely to require a high temperature than chicks of larger species. Few require a temperature above 33.3 to 35°C (92 to 95°F) after two weeks. However, it is very important to bear in mind that individuals, even of the same species, vary in their needs. Try to maintain the temperature at which the chicks appear most contented. When there are several in the brooder, perhaps of varying ages or species, the various chicks must be placed in the part of the brooder which suits them best.

Take into account that when underfloor heating is used the floor is the warmest part of the brooder. For chicks which require a lower temperature, raise the box off the floor. Also take into consideration where the light bulbs or heat source are placed and remember that the hottest part of the brooder will be above these (or below, with overhead heating).

To give greater temperature control in different parts of the brooder each light bulb can be controlled by an individual switch. However, it is not advisable to have only one light bulb switched on in a brooder containing young chicks, because if that bulb failed there would be no heat at all, and the chicks would die if this occurred overnight.

The use of two brooders is desirable for chicks of varying ages, rather than attempting to regulate the temperature in different parts of the brooder.

As chicks grow their need for warmth diminishes. On hatching, chicks of some species have some down, e.g. Cockatiels; a few are densely covered in down, e.g. lories and Grey Parrots. Most chicks lose this initial down by the age of two weeks or are very sparsely covered. Some chicks are naked on hatching, or almost so but for a few wisps, e.g. Ringneck Parrakeets and Amazon Parrots.

Most species start to acquire a second growth of down at about the age their eyes open, or later. For example, Eclectus Parrots acquire a woolly coat of dark grey down, most lories a layer of light grey down; cockatoos do not acquire second down and are naked when the quills break through.

Heavily-downed chicks may therefore require less heat as they grow. Eclectus Parrots, for example, retain their body temperature very well indeed, presumably because they make big weight gains at an early age and because they have a dense coat of down. In contrast, very small species may need the temperature maintained at 32.2°C (90°F) or even slightly higher for several weeks.

Some breeders like to cover over young chicks with cloth or paper towelling. I prefer to place small chicks in a very small box whose sides are cushioned with soft paper tissues so that the chicks fit snugly into the centre with little space to move around. I place a tissue over very young or very small chicks.

25

The importance of using an accurate thermometer cannot be stressed too strongly. The ideal is a digital thermometer which gives an instant reading; it is accurate and easy to read, but also rather expensive. It has a sensor attached so the actual thermometer does not need to be placed in the brooder. The model I use is the Diehl Thermotron.

Alternatively, you can use two ordinary thermometers in each brooder because if one is inaccurate chicks could die as a result. The thermometers should be placed where they can be read easily from outside the brooder and where they will not be soiled by chicks' droppings. Remember that the temperature will vary in different parts of the brooder and initially, after checking that both thermometers show the same reading, they should be moved to different parts of the brooder to find the warmest and coolest spots.

Mention must be made of the fact that small chicks lose body heat rapidly when removed for feeding. They should therefore be kept wrapped in a soft paper tissue and returned to the brooder as soon as possible.

Temperature is not the only environmental factor of importance. Humidity must also be considered. The atmosphere in a brooder of small chicks kept at a high temperature may be too dry unless a container of water is placed inside. The container is best built into the side of the brooder so that it cannot be spilled and can be replenished from outside. If this is not possible a heavy earthenware spill-proof container should be

*The interior of a brooder showing chick in plastic container, digital thermometer, combined thermometer and hygrometer, and a small dish of water.*

used; it must be shallow to prevent possible danger to chicks which may climb out of their box. Alternatively, one can use a jar of water, with the top protected or holes punched in the lid. It also provides an object against which chicks like to huddle and is therefore of some psychological value, especially to single chicks.

On no account should the humidity be so great that the sides of the brooder are covered in moisture as this could encourage the growth of mould (fungus), possibly with fatal consequences, if the sides of the brooder were not cleaned regularly.

If desired, a combined thermometer/hygrometer can be used, so that temperature and humidity can be read at a glance. The dial type, such as an inexpensive model called the Polymeter (available from Casella London Ltd, 109 Britannia Walk, London, N1), is excellent.

I have purposely avoided giving suggested temperatures for chicks of various species at differing ages. The great variety of circumstances plus the requirements of individual chicks makes the realisation that there can be no hard-and-fast rule very important.

By the time chicks are starting to feed on their own they are almost fully feathered, or are completely feathered. However, they may lose much weight during the weaning period (and always lose some weight), thus for some youngsters retaining heat over the weaning period can be of benefit. I have found this to be the case with the Tahiti Blue Lory (*Vini peruviana*), one of the smallest parrots in aviculture. There is often nothing to be gained by discontinuing heat too early – but perhaps everything to be lost.

The temperature should be adjusted downwards very gradually. In a temperate climate the stage is reached, usually when they are commencing to feed on their own, when heat is provided only at night, especially if the room is heated only during the daytime. The next step is to move the young to an unheated weaning cage.

To sum up, to assess whether a chick is being maintained at the correct temperature, there are three simple tests, as follows.

1) *Touch*. Feel how much warmth its body is emitting by holding it against your cheek immediately after removing it from the brooder.
2) *Observation*. Observe whether most of the time it is sleeping or resting contentedly. If it is very restless and/or extending the wings away from the body it is too hot. If it is so lethargic that it rarely moves it may be too cold. If it moves away from its siblings it may be too hot.
3) *Digestion*. If this is slow the temperature may be too low – but this would be more quickly evident from 1 and 2.

A warning: never adjust the temperature of a brooder late at night or just prior to leaving the house. The temperature control device on some brooders is not always as fine as one would desire. Incorrect adjustment could result in the death of chicks in a very short time. It is advisable to adjust the temperature in the morning because by the evening it should have found a constant level and chicks can be left overnight without fear of the temperature changing. Also, one has a chance to see whether the altered temperature is having a detrimental effect. Because of the danger of initial fluctuation, a brooder should be set up 24 hours before it will be required.

For about the first third of the nestling period chicks spend most of the time sleeping. Occasionally they adopt strange positions which could prove alarming to the uninitiated. They may lay outstretched, apparently scarcely breathing. How many breeders' hearts have missed a beat, after seeing a prone, inert chick, and fearing momentarily that it was dead? Older chicks of certain species, such as lories, may lay on their back or side; as they reach the weaning stage they become playful and apparently enjoy adopting strange positions. Chicks sleeping on their feet often let the neck sag onto the back, and their heads gradually fall forward. Alternatively, they may even lay down with legs outstretched behind them.

These apparently strange positions have no relevance to temperature, i.e. they are not caused by excessive or inadequate heating, but are quite normal for chicks kept in the correct temperature.

Finally, some advice on keeping very young chicks warm should they need to be transported by car. I believe the best method is to place them in a small cardboard, plastic or polystyrene box, on a bed of wood shavings and enclosed in a tissue with a light cloth or tissues over the chicks. Beneath the box place a hot water bottle. It is important to guard against over-heating in your anxiety to keep them warm. If no heat source is available, turn up the heat in the car and place the chicks in a soft paper tissue next to your body, such as inside your shirt.

# 4

# FEEDING –
# A PERSONAL VIEW

The two most crucial aspects of chick care are temperature and feeding; of the two, most mistakes occur with the latter. One could err with regard to food composition, consistency, food temperature and frequency of feeding, so there is a lot to be learned. Where parrot chicks are concerned, most mistakes occur with food content and consistency. Common errors are to feed very young chicks with over-rich diets and to give food which is too thick to chicks of all ages.

There are so many different diets and methods that the first-time hand-rearer is almost certain to become confused by what he has read or heard. The fact is that little is known about the dietary requirements of parrots or other altricial birds (those hatched blind and helpless). Nothing was known about their requirements for any amino acid, for example, until experiments were carried out at the Department of Avian Sciences at the University of California, Davis.

They designed a project to determine the quantitative lysine requirements of Cockatiel chicks (Grau and Roudybush, 1986). Lysine is an essential amino acid which cannot be manufactured within the bird but is deficient in cereals and in seeds commonly fed to birds. A deficiency may result in poor growth. In some species, in adults and young, a deficiency causes abnormal feather pigmentation, i.e. patches of light areas (yellow areas in green parrots, white areas in black birds, etc).

The basic approach at Davis was to feed Cockatiel chicks diets in which the amino acids were provided by mixtures of pure amino acids in place of protein. The lysine content of the diet could be varied and the effects on growth and feathering determined.

Those fed only 0.1 per cent lysine had a very poor growth and survival rate; it was much better in those fed 0.4 per cent until 14 days. The groups fed 1 or 2 per cent lysine survived and grew well but not as rapidly as similar chicks fed 20 per cent protein from isolated soybean protein supplemented with methionine. The group of chicks which had the

*Two Blue and Yellow Macaws (*Ara ararauna*), at 2 days (left) and 35 days.*

lysine content of the diet increased from 0.4 per cent to the 20 per cent protein diet at 14 days grew rapidly and continued to gain until they reached the expected fledging weight (80 to 90g). It was found that the lysine requirement of Cockatiel chicks hand-fed from hatching was 0.8 per cent of the dry portion of the diet. This diet, which contained amino acids equivalent to 20 per cent crude protein, was fed at 7 per cent solids for three days, then 30 per cent solids to weaning.

Feather pigmentation was normal at all lysine levels; thus the effects of lysine deficiency on the melanin formation in the feathers of Cockatiels appears to differ from that of many other birds.

The average breeder is not in a position to experiment with different components of the diet, and widely differing formulae prove successful. After the first few crucial days most parrot chicks prove quite easy to rear, provided that the diet is not so rich that it causes damage to the liver and kidneys or that it is not deficient in biotin, one of the B-complex vitamins. Both cause fatty liver and kidney syndrome (FLKS).

## A SIMPLE BASIC DIET

Over the years I experimented with diets until I found one which was quick and easy to prepare and which suited a wide range of parrot species. In my early years of hand-rearing I reached a situation where two or three different formulae had to be heated at each feed for different species. This was time-consuming and inconvenient so, with my former husband, Bob Grantham, I found a simple basic diet which suited all species and which could easily be adapted for older chicks. It did away with the use of a food mixer or grinder, except the latter to grind up sunflower seed kernels.

For years, the basic diet I have used consists of equal parts of two types of Heinz tinned baby foods: Pure Fruit (in recent years this has replaced Fruit Dessert) and Bone and Beef Broth with Vegetables. I believe that fruit is an important aid to digestion and that all parrot chicks should have some fruit in their diet. A common problem is a compacted crop; it is soon evident that food is not passing out of the crop. There are a number of reasons: an over-rich diet leading to liver failure; food fed too thick; or incorrect content. The problem is unlikely to arise when a large proportion of the food consists of Pure Fruit. It is as its name suggests – pure fruit with nothing added. The protein content is very low (just over 2 per cent). If the tinned baby food is not available an apple, pear or banana can be placed in a blender to produce a similar food, after the fruit has been peeled.

Those who are hand-rearing a large number of chicks will find it too expensive to purchase tinned products, as will breeders who have access to a free or inexpensive source of cultivated and wild fruits. A wide variety can be used to make the fruit content of the baby food. The resulting 'cocktail' gives more variety than found in tinned products. An example is as follows: peel three apples, one pear, half an orange, half a pomegranate and half a banana, and place in a blender with a handful of blackberries and a bunch of elderberries. It is not necessary to add water. Almost any combination of fruits can be used, as well as vegetables, such as carrot, spinach and kale. Enough can be made to last a couple of days, if refrigerated.

I have not tried to simulate the other component, Bone and Beef Broth with Vegetables. It is one of a large range of baby dinners. Probably the others are equally good – I have not used them, because, having found a successful food, I have no reason to change it. The protein content of the Bone and Beef Broth is shown on the label as 4 per cent. This appears low on a percentage basis but because the water content is high, it contains about 26 per cent of the total energy (calories) as protein. The mixture therefore contains about 14 per cent of its energy in the form of protein.

## PROTEIN

The percentage of energy as protein required by parrot chicks is unknown. Studies of dietary requirements for domestic animals and human babies are advanced because they are financed by industry. As Professor T. G. Taylor of the University of Southampton pointed out to me:

'The percentage of energy as protein required by any species is related to its rate of growth, i.e. the rate at which it stores protein in its tissues. Human babies grow slowly and breast milk contains about 6 per cent of its energy as protein; calves grow much faster and cow's milk contains about 20 per cent protein energy. Chicks of the domestic fowl are fed on diets with about 25 per cent and turkeys about 33 per cent of protein energy.

'One can only guess at the percentage of energy as protein that parrot chicks require. All species will require less protein as they grow older, i.e. their greatest requirements for protein will be at hatching.

'If a diet contains really excessive amounts of protein, the kidneys will certainly be over-strained and they may have difficulty in secreting all the uric acid produced. The fatty-liver-kidney syndrome, however, appears to be caused by a deficiency of the vitamin biotin. The main effect of a diet too low in protein, and therefore high in carbohydrate and fat, is poor growth.'

The energy as protein requirements of different species probably differ. It would appear to me that fruit- and nectar-feeders require less protein than species such as the Budgerigar which exist predominantly on seed. When Professor Taylor analysed the crop content of Budgerigar chicks he found it contained 20–25 per cent of its energy as protein. On the single occasion on which I attempted to rear Cockatiel chicks from the egg on the above diet for the first few days only, their growth rate was very poor. Also, one often hears of Cockatiels and Australian Parrakeets being reared on little else than baby cereal. This does not suit parrots which are not predominantly seedeaters (Low, 1977).

Why is this? Is it related to their natural diet or is it connected with the fact that energy as protein requirements are related to the rate of growth of the species. It so happens that parrots which are primarily seedeaters in the wild (there are few), mainly Cockatiels and Australian Parrakeets, spend only four or five weeks in the nest, while those whose natural diet is mainly fruit, vegetable matter and nectar spend at least eight weeks in the nest, an average of ten weeks and upward of three months in a few cases.

It was apparent that different parrot species have varying requirements for protein, and that failure to provide the correct level at an early age results in the chick's death. However, it was not until Professor

Taylor pointed out to me that energy as protein requirements are related to growth rate that I realised it should be easy to work out the requirements of any species, assuming it is known how long the young normally remain in the nest.

Budgerigars spend about four weeks in the nest and, as Professor Taylor indicated, have energy as protein requirements of 20 to 25 per cent. Amazons and conures spend about eight weeks in the nest and appear to have energy as protein needs of about 12 per cent. Large cockatoos, Eclectus and other birds which spend more than ten weeks in the nest probably require no more than about 10 per cent protein.

## CALCIUM

Once the first two crucial weeks have passed parrot chicks appear less vulnerable to mistakes in their diet. After about ten days the food can gradually be supplemented with ground up sunflower seed (about 24 per cent protein, dry weight) and wheat germ cereal (similar protein content).

For the first ten days or so my parrot chicks (which do not include Cockatiels and Australian Parrakeets) receive nothing but the two types of baby foods described, mixed with water and a small amount of sterilised bone flour, and/or a calcium and Vitamin $D_3$ supplement of some kind. The latter is given because calcium deficiency, which usually has tragic consequences for chicks of all species, is common. Probably this deficiency is responsible for more breeding failures than any other component of the diet. If a laying female is short of calcium the eggs will be soft-shelled or otherwise malformed and laying them may cost her her life. If the chicks are short of calcium they will have rickets and be crippled for life or have to be destroyed at an early age.

These days calcium supplements are easy to obtain and to use, thus there is no excuse for such tragedies. During the breeding season I give the liquid calcium and Vitamin D supplement Collo-Cal D (C-Vet Ltd, Bury St Edmunds, Suffolk, UK) in bread and milk to all females before and during laying and when they are rearing young. (In the USA breeders use Super-Hygliceron B.) Chicks being hand-reared have calcium in two forms: a powdered supplement such as MSA in the Nekton range (available worldwide) and an occasional drop of Collo-Cal D on to the spoon after the food has been heated. Vitamin D is required for absorption of calcium, and is contained in Collo-Cal D, available from veterinarians. Another source of calcium is sterilised bone flour.

The calcium requirements of chicks of large species are greater than those of small species. This is because in proportion to their body weight they need and have larger bones.

## BACTERIA

It is generally thought that parrot chicks require a supplement to provide them with bacteria if they have never been fed by their parents or any other birds. In the past I used natural (live) yoghurt. A small amount (unheated) was placed on the spoon immediately before the chick was fed. This was offered several times a day for four or five days. Yoghurt is basically soured milk and an excellent source of vitamins, minerals and proteins. 'Live' yoghurt, in contrast to ultra-heat treated (UHT), contains bacteria which would be killed by heat treatment given to UHT. However, it is doubtful whether, as a result of giving parrot chicks live yoghurt, bacteria would be established in the intestines.

Professor Taylor pointed out to me that live yoghurt provides a source of lactobacillus which, in human babies, inhabits the lower intestines and creates an acid environment (by converting lactose to lactic acid). This serves to discourage harmful bacteria. In parrots, however, this bacterium is unlikely to be established in the lower intestines unless chicks were given milk, because lactobacilli need lactose to live on. He suspects that parrot chicks acquire an appropriate bacterial flora from their environment.

In the USA powdered acidophilus is used by some breeders; this is a species of lactobacillus that inhabits the gut of babies. It is sold in health food shops (e.g. Lactinex Granules). In the opinion of Professor Taylor, however, it has no particular value for people or for birds.

He also pointed out that milk-based foods are unsuitable for rearing chicks of all kinds because they are deficient in the amino acid arginine relative to lysine. Arginine is an essential amino acid for birds but not for mammals. When chicks are given casein (such as in some high-protein human foods) as the sole source of protein they grow very poorly. This deficiency can be overcome by mixing casein with gelatine, but carbohydrate, fat, minerals and vitamins would have to be added in order to make a complete diet.

In theory egg is the best form of protein. Professor Taylor suggested that egg custard could be tried as a component of the food mixture.

## METHOD OF FEEDING

To recap, the food I offer very young chicks consists of the two types of baby food, plus a calcium supplement, and water. The amount of water is decreased as the chicks mature. The initial feeds must be of a very thin consistency – thinner than milk. The amount which can be given to a newly-hatched chick is minute. It is for this reason that they need to be fed frequently – if possible, a little every hour. If this is out of the question, a frequency of one-and-a-half to two hours will suffice. A newly-hatched chick can swallow only slowly, it quickly tires and loses heat away from the brooder and its crop capacity is minute. A tiny chick should be wrapped in a soft paper tissue to prevent loss of body heat, especially on contact with cold hands, and to ensure that no food falls on it. Hands should be warmed before picking up a chick, if necessary. When feeding chicks of different ages, the smallest should be fed first because it loses body heat more quickly than its larger companions. Also, as the food cools it becomes less attractive to young chicks.

## FOOD PREPARATION

As chicks mature they will take food cooler; but very young chicks do need the food hot and fed from a warm feeding implement. It is vitally important to note, however, that chicks can be killed by food which is scalding hot. If fed such food too often the interior of the crop can be burned to the degree that it actually bursts open. I have heard of this happening. The oesophagus must also become burned and feeding must be a horribly painful process for a tiny, helpless chick.

Before offering food *always* test it by dropping a little on to one's finger or by using either a cook's thermometer or the digital thermometer referred to earlier, in which the probe can be inserted into the food. The latter should be inserted for at least two-thirds of its length for approximately 30 seconds in the Diehl Thermotron which I use. The temperature should be in the region of 43°C (110°F) for very young chicks, slightly less for older chicks.

Food should be prepared fresh daily, unless a large batch is made and frozen for future use. If it is kept in the saucepan in which it is heated, evaporation means that a small amount of water will need to be added at each feed or by the end of the day it will be unacceptably thick.

## FREQUENCY OF FEEDING

My own feeding schedule for chicks commences daily at 6.30 am; the last feed is given about 11.30 pm. In addition, all chicks under one week old, and those of very small species for a few days more, are given a 3 am feed. After a week or so this is extended gradually to 4 am, 5 am and 6 am, until it synchronises with the older chicks.

One hears of newly-hatched chicks being fed every two hours throughout the day and night. This is definitely not necessary and causes much stress to the feeder who will be exhausted after two or three nights. A 3 am feed ensures that the chick has sufficient liquid intake to last it several hours and that it will not become dehydrated. This fact and ensuring that the temperature suits it are the two reasons for the 3 am

*Grey Parrot chicks (*Psittacus erithacus*) soon after hatching. The down on the body of the right-hand chick has not yet dried out.*

feed. It it not necessary for a chick to receive food around the clock and it would not have done so had it been left with its parents. It is not true, however, that parrots do not feed their young during the hours of darkness. Many do feed their young during the night. This is particularly easy to ascertain in cockatoos in which the sound made by the chick as it receives food is extremely far-carrying. Probably, however, many young parrots fed at night receive minimal amounts of food.

In hand-reared chicks the danger of dehydration occurs because they are being kept at a constant high temperature and perhaps in a more drying type of heat than that provided by the parents. I keep a small container of water in the brooder and humidity varies between 40 and 60 per cent.

On the first night that chicks spend in the brooder checking the temperature at 3 am is equally as important as feeding. Chicks left several hours in an incorrect temperature could be dead by 6.30 am.

On the second day the feeding frequency for all chicks except those under about 4 g can be extended to between one-and-a-half to two hours, and for smaller chicks, if possible, between one and one-and-a-half hours. The liquid consistency of the food means that it passes through the crop in perhaps less than one hour; the next feed should be given when the crop is empty or when it has been empty for up to an hour; but *not* when there is still food in the crop. By allowing the crop to empty you will know the rate at which food is being digested. The first sign that something is wrong is usually that the crop is not empty after the normal period. This subject and how to deal with it are covered in the following chapter. Some breeders advocate that a chick's crop must never be allowed to empty when it is very young. I disagree totally with this and feel that chicks fed in this way are likely candidates for fatty liver and kidney syndrome. They are *too* well fed and the excess food may be stored in the liver as fat, and before very long causes the chick's death.

It is important that a feeding schedule is adhered to rigidly. You must acquire the habit of feeding chicks on the hour or the half-hour, for example, so that you know when the next feed is due by glancing at the clock. If irregular feeding times occur the feeder will be unable to remember when the next feed is due unless the time of each feed is written down. Alternatively, when each feed is finished, you can look at the clock and make a mental note of the hour the next feed is due. It is better not to trust to memory, however.

Regular feeding times are important not because a chick *must* receive food every two hours, or whatever the frequency, but because it is

*Most parrot chicks have large feet which seem out of proportion to their bodies until they are almost fully grown. A Lesser (Timor) Sulphur-crested Cockatoo (*Cacatua sulphurea*), nearly six weeks old, is shown here.*

essential to develop a strict routine. This is especially the case with a single chick or one without a nest-mate, because you cannot assess whether a half-full crop when you expect it to be empty is due to failure to note when the last feed was given or due to something being wrong with the chick – and no sibling for comparison.

As a chick grows the interval between feeds can be extended because its crop expands and its capacity increases. Also, slightly thicker food will be taken which is not digested as quickly as that of a more liquid consistency. However, in my opinion the amount of food given should not exceed that which takes three hours to pass through the crop.

Until they approach weaning age I feed chicks every two-and-a-half to three hours (every two hours for tiny species which weigh less than 40 g when adult), not filling their crops to capacity. I feel that this is preferable to feeding chicks every four hours and filling them until their crops bulge. The danger in this practice is that, on the very rare occasions when it might be necessary to empty the crop, this would prove more difficult; also, if a chick had digestive problems and its crop was emptying abnormally slowly, it would take much longer to do so and the risk of the crop contents becoming sour would be greatly increased.

## AMOUNT OF FOOD TO FEED TO CHICKS

It is often difficult for a beginner to know how much food to give. There is no rule which can be applied, such as a proportion of the chick's weight. The amount given varies according to the age (a smaller proportion relevant to body weight is taken by newly-hatched chicks and those approaching weaning), consistency of the food, crop capacity etc, as well as the inclination of the feeder. I have seen chicks given twice the amount of food which I personally would have offered.

As a guide, refer to Fig. 10, drawn up as the result of measuring the amount of food given at one feed daily to a Grey Parrot chick, by weighing the chick before and after feeding.

Here are some random weights of chicks I have hand-reared,

| Species | Age (days) | Weight | Quantity |
|---|---|---|---|
| Goldie's Lorikeet | 27 | 34 g | 3 g |
| (*Trichoglossus goldiei*) | 34 | 40 g | 4 g |
| Meyer's Lorikeet | 37 | 33 g | 3.5 g |
| (*Trichoglossus flavoviridis meyeri*) | 39 | 34.5 g | 2.5 g |
| Iris Lorikeet | 11 | 17 g | 1 g |
| (*Trichoglossus iris*) | 23 | 30 g | 3.5 g |
| | 34 | 43 g | 4.5 g |

| Species | Age (days) | Weight | Quantity |
|---|---|---|---|
| Tahiti Blue Lory | 53 | 18.5 g | 2.5 g |
| (Vini peruviana) | | | |
| Cruentata Conure | ? | 77 g | 6 g |
| (Pyrrhura cruentata) | ? | 89 g | 6 g |
| Lesser (Timor) | | | |
| Sulphur-crested Cockatoo | 15 | 52 g | 4 g |
| (Cacatua sulphurea) | | | |
| Black-capped Lory | 14 | 32.5 g | 5.5 g |
| (Lorius lory lory) | 24 | 79 g | 7 g |
| Forsten's Lorikeet | 14 | 13 g | 2.5 g |
| (Trichoglossus haematodus forsteni) | 24 | 34.5 g | 6 g |
| Dusky Lory | 24 | 66 g | 7 g |
| (Pseudeos fuscata) | 44 | 112 g | 8 g |
| | 64 | 124 g | 12 g |
| Umbrella Cockatoo | 9 | 55 g | 5 g |
| (Cacatua alba) | 15 | 90 g | 10 g |

showing their weight and the quantity of good given at one feed.

Beware over-feeding! Most chicks, except older ones, definitely do not know when they have had enough and will continue to accept food when the crop is bulging dangerously. Over-feeding is much more harmful than under-feeding. If in doubt regarding the quantity to give at each feed, err towards the minimum, not the maximum.

Over-feeding results in the crop being stretched. In some chicks the pendulous shape of the crop can cause problems in that it may not empty completely; food remains in the bottom of the crop and becomes sour. This is not necessarily due to the crop being stretched by over-feeding but perhaps is more likely to occur in this case.

## FEEDING RESPONSE

At this point reference should be made to the feeding response of parrot chicks. Even before their eyes open, chicks respond to the touch of the warm spoon on the lower mandible by gripping it between the mandibles and pumping the head up and down, as the food is swallowed. Newly-hatched chicks will not do this for some hours or even two or three days, depending on their strength. They take food from the spoon by sucking and it may only be by watching the throat movement that one is aware that food is being swallowed. The degree of vigour of the pumping movement varies in individuals of the same species, and also with species. It is, for example, very strong in cockatoos and weak in Eclectus Parrots.

## THE CROP

After the food is swallowed it travels down to the crop. Some newcomers to hand-rearing do not know which part of the chick's anatomy is the crop. The food can be seen usually travelling down the right side of the neck, in an unfeathered chick, and filling the area in front of or immediately below the chest. The crop extends slightly backwards to the right side of the neck in many chicks (see Fig. 2).

Crop shapes differ not only with the species but even in individuals. In some birds the crop is slung lower and expands widthways, though in most it bulges out well in front of the chick. With very young chicks in which the skin is almost transparent one can see the food travelling down into the crop.

It is easy to test the consistency of the food within the crop by gently feeling the area, if necessary. Rarely, hard lumps of food can form (could this be due to the water content of the food being too low?). In chicks in the nest, one can feel or even see whole sunflower kernels. Some females will pack the crop of a chick with them, possibly with disastrous results as they are difficult for young chicks to digest.

The amount of food which is fed by its natural parent is not necessarily a good guide as to how much a chick should be offered. My Dusky Lories (*Pseudeos fuscata*) generally favour one chick, which will be seen with a balloon-like crop, while its unfortunate sibling is poorly fed and, on occasions, has required supplementary feeding.

*Fig. 2   Nestling showing position of crop.*

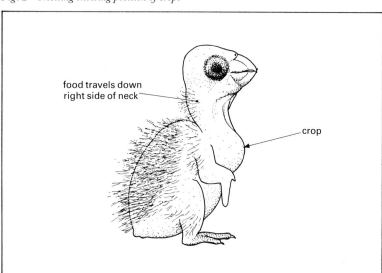

food travels down
right side of neck

crop

## FOOD CONDITION

Whatever the circumstances, attention must be paid to the condition of the food offered. It is advisable to place it in a refrigerator between feeds in warm weather. Any food left at the end of the day (or after 24 hours) should be discarded, and fresh food made.

## HEATING FOOD

Food is heated by stirring in a small saucepan over a low heat. If only a small amount needs to be heated, the lower half of the type of egg poacher made in two sections can be used. Alternatively, food can be heated by placing it in a glass container within a saucepan of boiling water. The saucepan can be taken to the table, or wherever feeding is carried out, and the food will keep warm longer. This is recommended when feeding a large number of chicks, to prevent the food becoming cool and unacceptable to the last to be fed. If a chick's refusal of food is instant it is normally because the food has cooled unacceptably.

Another method of heating food which is most useful to those feeding a large number of chicks is the microwave oven. It can be used to re-heat cooling food very quickly. However, food must be stirred thoroughly to ensure that there are no hot spots.

## FEEDING IMPLEMENTS

Probably the instrument most often used for feeding chicks is a syringe, but I have always used a teaspoon with the sides bent inwards. For newly-hatched chicks a suitably adapted plastic spoon can be used, as plastic is a softer material. Plastic spoons obviously have a short life-span, so several should be shaped as required by holding them in a flame or exposing them to a high temperature. A pair of pliers can be used to bend metal spoons. In my opinion, a spoon is the ideal implement, except for the person who has a large number of chicks to feed.

I prefer the spoon to other implements because the chick helps itself, almost as it would from its parent's beak. The smallest chick will feed readily provided that the spoon (and the food) are warm. The spoon retains heat longer than the top layer of food; so, when testing the temperature of the food with the tongue, also test the spoon, to ensure it will not burn the chick.

The fact that the spoon is larger than the chick does not matter! I have had newly hatched Tahiti Blue Lories (*Vini peruviana*) weighing 2 g feeding from a teaspoon in which they could sit with ease (Low, 1985).

The spoon is not practical in all circumstances. If a chick is too weak to

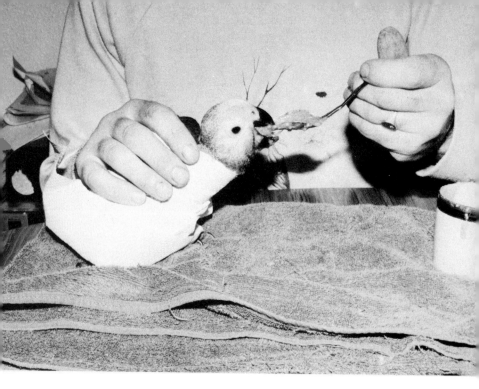

*A bent teaspoon is used by the author for feeding chicks. Paper towel wrapped around the front of the chick prevents food falling on its plumage.*

help itself, an eye dropper is recommended, or a dropper used with certain brands of liquid multivitamins (e.g. Abdec). When a chick is removed from the nest well after its eyes have opened, and it is partly or wholly feathered, initially it will have to be syringe-fed because it will not willingly take food. In these circumstances, chicks demonstrate fear. This varies according to the species. Some will lunge at the hands and others will hiss or attempt to bite initially. Spoon-feeding will not be possible until they have lost their fear – after three or four days or more.

Incidentally, the actual process of removing the chicks from the nest can be difficult in the case of some of the larger parrots, either because they are very aggressive or because the female rarely leaves the nest or is quick to return when she does. For this reason the nest-box should be situated on the outside of the aviary, and a piece of tin should be dropped over the entrance as soon as the female vacates the nest, if necessary attaching string to the tin and operating it from a distance.

# 5

# OTHER FEEDING METHODS

In devoting a chapter to my own feeding method it was not intended to convey that this is the best. Many methods are successful; the one I used is described fully because a book on hand-feeding must be empirical, i.e. written as the result of personal experience. There is no substitute. Other methods must also be described, though, because that which suits one person or one species may not suit another.

Two points must be emphasised, however: never change a successful

*Scarlet Macaw (*Ara macao) *on the day it hatched.*

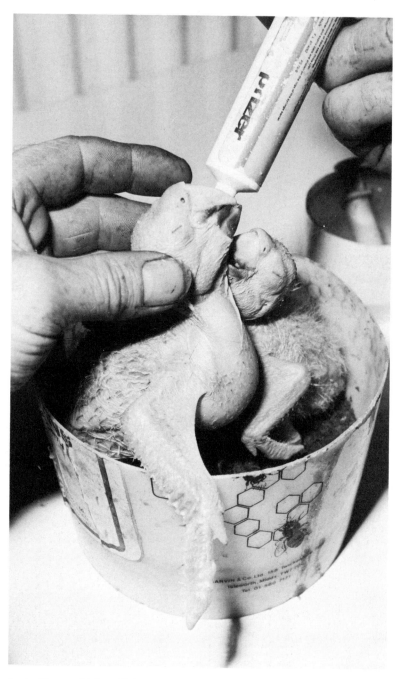

*Scarlet Macaws, 21 days old, being fed by syringe.*

*Scarlet Macaw at 30 days.*

*Scarlet Macaw at 45 days.*

method for the sake of experimentation; and never drastically alter a chick's diet unless there is a very good reason. When you have found a good method, stick to it. Do not be tempted to change your formula or routine as the result of reading about or seeing another person's method unless you are not satisfied with your results. Even then do not make changes for change's sake, but consider carefully what benefit there is in adopting a different approach.

## SYRINGES AND OTHER FEEDING IMPLEMENTS

First, consider the alternative implements to the spoon. The most popular is the plastic disposable syringe from which the needle has been removed. Such syringes can be obtained from chemists and veterinarians. Syringe feeding has the advantage of speed – and no other advantage, in my opinion. The main disadvantage is the danger of killing a chick if food enters the windpipe. This has happened on countless occasions. Death is sudden. In depressing the plunger of the syringe, one cannot always control the direction of the food, especially if the chick moves suddenly. When a spoon is used, the chick takes the food from the spoon and swallows readily. In using a syringe, initially a little food should be squirted on to the chick's tongue and, when it swallows it, the chick should begin to move its head up and down, 'pumping' as it would if fed by the parent. When this occurs the tube is directed to the back of the throat and the food released. Some breeders insert the tube down the throat and into the crop. As chicks grow, the size of the tube on the syringe should be increased. If it is thicker than the windpipe, there should be no danger of the young bird choking.

It must be noted that the nozzle of the syringe is covered with soft rubber, such as surgical tubing, bicycle valve rubber or the type formerly used to cover flex wire (not the hard plastic now in use). The ideal length of the rubber tubing is short, i.e. about 2.5 cm (1 in).

When a syringe is used the food must be of a fairly thin consistency unless the nozzle is wide. It must be thoroughly washed after each feed and all surplus food removed. Before using the syringe it must be warmed by standing it in a cup of hot water; the food has previously been heated. If the syringe is cold small chicks will refuse to feed.

As spoon-feeding is not always possible or practical, breeders who normally use a spoon may need to employ a syringe in certain circumstances. Young removed from the nest when well-feathered and approaching weaning age display fear initially and will seldom feed from a spoon. A syringe is then essential. Spoon-feeding is not practical in the case of very large parrots such as macaws, after they are a couple of weeks old. They consume large amounts at each feed and spoon-feeding would be very time-consuming. A useful implement to feed such youngsters is a meat baster, which looks like a very large syringe.

Some strange implements have been employed to feed parrot chicks, such as a wooden spatula or even, unbelievably, a knitting needle! However, this is not necessary. Every household possesses a teaspoon!

## SPECIFIC DIET FORMULAE

Having covered alternative feeding implements, I will now describe various diets. It would be possible to fill an entire book with formulae used for hand-feeding parrot chicks. However, it should be borne in mind that because a certain diet results in young being reared does not necessarily mean that it is successful. Only if the young are healthy can it be judged so. On more than one occasion I have heard of the death of a young hand-reared parrot several months after it has been sold. Post-mortem examination has revealed that the liver was diseased as the result of the bird being incorrectly fed.

Beware of diets which are over-rich or indigestible, as these probably account for the majority of deaths of hand-fed parrots, and not necessarily during the period of hand-rearing. Death can occur some months afterwards if the chick has suffered liver damage due to an incorrect diet.

An example of unsuitable food for an Amazon (it might suffice for an Australian parrakeet) was the baby cereal and ground sunflower seed kernels given to a newly-hatched Yellow-billed (*Amazona collaria*). The chick was unable to digest this food properly. Fortunately, the mistake was rectified quickly and the chick was reared. Fruit is a vital component of the diet for nearly all species, in my opinion, as it is an invaluable aid to digestion. In this respect, papaya is second to none.

If the diet is obviously unsuitable and it is necessary to seek advice, try to find someone with experience who has been using the same food over a fair period with good results. Avoid diets suggested by people who are continually changing or experimenting with the food because this means that they have yet to find a satisfactory formula.

All the diets described below have been proved successful over a number of years.

### San Diego Zoo – Lories

The institute which can be said to have pioneered the hand-rearing of parrots and other birds was San Diego Zoo in California, under the curatorship of K. C. Lint, one of the world's finest curators of birds. He commenced hand-rearing in the 1930s, forty years or so before it became a common practice. As an example, between 1929 and 1970 a pair of

Bare-eyed Cockatoos (*Cacatua sanguinea*) there produced 103 young, all or most of which were hand-reared.

K. C. Lint was my mentor and teacher. When I visited San Diego Zoo in 1974 he showed me the procedure for hand-rearing parrot chicks, at a time when no one in the UK was regularly carrying this out. His help and advice gave me the courage to remove my first chicks from the nest at a time when chicks were hand-raised only in an emergency.

To this day many parrots, including rare species such as the Pesquet's, described elsewhere in this chapter, are hand-reared at San Diego Zoo. These include lories. San Diego's formula for hand-rearing these birds is as follows: to a pint of water which has been brought up to the boil are added 48 g of wheat hearts (wheat germ cereal), 40 g of dark Karo syrup and 12 g of trout pellets. These are mixed together and boiled until the wheat germ cereal is cooked (three to five minutes).

When the mixture has cooled one egg yolk is added which has been mixed with 50 ml of water. This is stirred well then 30 g of a special premix is added. This consists of: 200 g of Gevral Protein (a protein-mineral concentrate by Lederle Laboratories Division, American Cyanamid Co, Pearl River, NY 10965, USA); 100 g of Hydramin; 5 g of Vitamycin (Vionate) (E. R. Suibb & Sons Inc, Princeton, New Jersey 08540, USA, and Regal House, Twickenham, Middlesex TW1 3QT, UK); 3 g of iodised salt, 0.6 g of L-Cystine and 0.5 g of calcium lactate.

Added to this is one large lettuce leaf and the whole is then mixed in a blender.

The nutrient composition of this food is as follows: protein 28.4 per cent; ME (metabolisable energy) 3430 kcal/kg; calcium 0.62 per cent; phosphorus 0.5 per cent; lysine 1.5 per cent; methionine 0.58 per cent; cystine 0.43 per cent.

## Patricia King – Lories

In the UK a most successful breeder of *Eos* and *Chalcopsitta* lories is Mrs Patricia King of Cornwall, who hatches all the eggs in an incubator and hand-rears the young. The diet used is as follows: on day one, diluted Cow and Gate (US equivalent Gerber's) Fruit Delight baby food; day two, a mixture of Fruit Delight, natural yoghurt, one teaspoonful of baby cereal and half a teaspoonful of wheat germ cereal granules. On day three onwards, nectar, as fed to the adult birds, is added to the diet. This consists of equal parts of honey, Complan (invalid liquid diet, Glaxo-Farley Foods Ltd, Plymouth, Devon, UK) and Horlicks.

## Velma Hart – Amazons

In the USA many diets are based on that originally used by the late Mrs Velma Hart in California, who was a pioneer of hand-rearing. In the

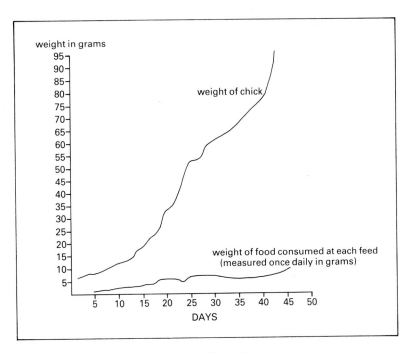

Fig. 3   Development of Blue-streaked Lory (Eos reticulata).

Fig. 4   Development of Blue-streaked (-----) and Forsten's (———) Lories hand-reared simultaneously.

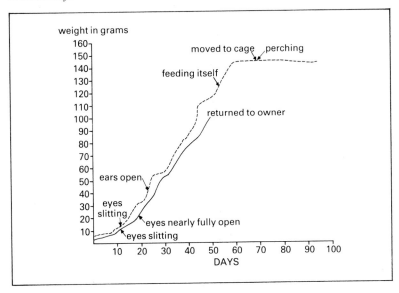

1950s she was rearing Amazons on a mixture consisting of one-third raw egg yolk and one teaspoonful each of pablum, white cornflour and wheat germ. This was moistened with hot water and cooked. After two weeks the egg yolk was eliminated and ground dog kibble was added.

## Ramon Noegel and Greg Moss – Amazons

Among the most successful breeders currently in the USA are Ramon Noegel and Greg Moss, who specialise in breeding endangered species of Amazon parrots. Their basic diet is that described above; also added are cooked brown rice, fresh carrots, frozen green peas and sweetcorn, ripe banana, ripe papaya, apple and other fruit, and two eggs. All this is cooked in a large pot with a little corn syrup and corn oil, and blended well. High-protein baby foods and Gerber's baby foods (in jars) (Gerber Products Co, Fremont, Michigan 49412, USA), such as beetroot and squash (courgettes) are added before the food is used. The uneaten food is refrigerated and new food made up every other day.

Corn oil and corn syrup are not commonly used in hand-rearing formulae outside the USA but Ramon Noegel pointed out: 'Fat is necessary for lubrication and avoids blockage in the crop and intestines.' Papaya is an especially beneficial food for it contains enzymes which aid digestion. It can therefore be recommended for a chick whose crop is slow to empty.

By 1985 Ramon Noegel had been hand-rearing endangered parrots for more than a decade – longer than anyone else. In a letter to me, written that year, he related: 'Most of the better aviculturists in the States still ascribe to Velma Hart's formula – they have had to return to it after some tragic experiences. Some swear by one formula and get good results while others use the same and do not. The reasons may be several fold: the conditions in which they are kept (temperate or tropical climate), the attitude of the keeper, the instrument being used to feed the young and the strength of the chick when it hatched. The species is also relevant. Special birds like Hawk-heads and Golden (Queen of Bavaria's) Conures must have a bland diet for the initial two or three weeks, while Amazons, conures in general and macaws seem to thrive on almost any formula.'

Ramon Noegel has found, however, that Hyacinthine Macaws also fall into the category of chicks which need special treatment, being much more sensitive when hand-reared from day one than Scarlets or Blue and Yellow Macaws. Their crops usually empty more slowly, the chicks grow more slowly and require more heat until they are feathered. He wrote (1982): 'One of the most important considerations is not to fill the crop full. Since they are eager to feed, this is hard to refrain from doing. It is better to under-feed and feed more often when the crop is empty. Always keep the crop loose so that the normal constrictions can occur or an impacted and sour crop will result and the chick will soon die.'

Ramon Noegel mentioned 'the attitude of the keeper' – something which is not often taken into consideration. Yet it is of the greatest importance. Chicks of the more intelligent species respond to a caring attitude, just as human babies do. Perhaps all parrot species do; but the bond between bird and feeder is less evident in some.

Certain species, especially those in which a strong pair bond is evident in adults, such as the larger lories, Queen of Bavaria's Conures and macaws, crave affection. The psychological benefits of a feeder who returns that affection must be immense. A caring attitude should *never* be underestimated.

### Wayne and Annabelle Schulenburg – Pesquet's Parrot

As pointed out by Ramon Noegel, the requirements of various species do differ, especially the dietary needs. The highly unusual Pesquet's Parrot (*Psittrichas fulgidus*), one of the most distinctive members of the parrot family, does not eat seed. This very large black and red bird exists principally on soft fruits and berries; many other parrots do but in confinement most can be persuaded to sample seed. This is not the case with this species or with some lories.

Pesquet's Parrot has rarely been bred in captivity but at San Diego Zoo ten or so young were produced from one pair in 1984 and 1986. The chicks were hand-reared at her home by Annabelle Schulenburg, wife of one of the keepers, Wayne Schulenburg. I am indebted to him for providing details of their diet and methods.

The chicks were hatched at the zoo and transferred to the Schulenburg household for their first feed, which consists of yoghurt and water. At the third feed Gerber's baby egg yolk is added; for the fifth feed unsweetened apple sauce and brown sugar was included. This is the diet for the next three days.

On the fourth day the basic formula is given. 9 kg (20 lbs) are made at once, most of which is placed in butter tubs and frozen, to be used as required. The formula is composed of the following items: 6.7 kg (15 lbs) of masa herina (tortilla corn flour), four baby food jars each of green beans, peas, spinach, corn, carrots and apple sauce, also eight egg yolks, 900 g (32 oz) of raw wheat germ, 1 kg (36 oz) of light molasses, 900 g (32 oz) of non-fat instant dry milk and 900 g (32 oz) of peanut butter. All except the masa are mixed together. Equal parts of masa, the above mixture and water are placed in a blender and mixed. When the chicks' pin feathers start to erupt, mashed banana is added to the diet. The diet is adapted for species other than Pesquet's Parrots and lories by adding ground millet and sunflower kernels when the feathers start to erupt.

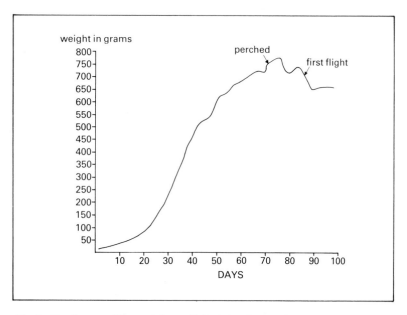

*Fig. 5   Development of Pesquet's Parrot (*Psittrichas fulgidus*) hatched at San Diego Zoo on 15 March 1984 and hand-reared.*

From the fifth day the Pesquet's chicks are fed every three hours and the temperature is reduced to 34.4°C (94°F) from 35°C (95°F). They are then removed from a Marsh Farms Turn-X incubator to an aquarium brooder.

From the tenth day the chicks are fed every four hours. From day 12 onwards the egg yolk and yoghurt are omitted from the diet and tinned milk is added. From two weeks the diet includes a multi-vitamin mixture and strained baby banana.

Frequency of feeding is reduced to between four-and-a-quarter and five hours in these large birds at four weeks old, when they take one-quarter of a cupful of food at each feed. From the 32nd day the chicks are fed only four times daily. On day 39 strained baby banana is eliminated from the diet and replaced with mashed banana. Three days later the food intake is increased to half a cup per feed.

On the 50th day chicks are moved to a brooder cage heated by a softly-coloured light bulb. On the 62nd day a bowl of soft fruit is offered. By the 80th day they are fed only twice daily as much fruit is eaten.

For comparison with development in other species, it is useful to know that Pesquet's chicks perch at 70 days and take their first flight aged between 84 and 89 days. Few people will be hand-rearing Pesquet's Parrots, but they can apply the above information to other species.

## Robbie Harris – Conures

Aviculturists are more likely to be rearing conures, the parrakeets from South and Central America of which many species breed readily in captivity. Robbie Harris, in California, hand-feeds large numbers of these and other neotropical parrots. On occasions they have been feeding as many as 80 chicks. Their success rate is high and they have gained several awards for breeding species for the first time in the USA.

For chicks older than four days the Harrises use the following formula. One tablespoonful each of corn oil and honey, plus half a teaspoonful of salt, are added to five cups of water. One cup of oatmeal and half a cup each of wheat hearts (wheat germ cereal) and high-protein baby cereal are added, stirring continuously to prevent lumps forming. This food is cooked for three to five minutes after it boils. Then one 4½-oz jar of each of the following baby foods are added: creamed spinach, strained peas, strained carrots, creamed corn, apple sauce and banana, also half a cup of corn (maize) meal (optional), one cup of powdered milk and two cups of sunflower meal. All are stirred until well blended.

The sunflower meal is prepared by putting sunflower kernels in a blender with two slices of dried wheat bread broken up into crumbs (to prevent the sunflower from becoming sticky). It is blended until very fine.

*Hawk-headed Parrot (*Deroptyus accipitrinus*) at 1 day.*

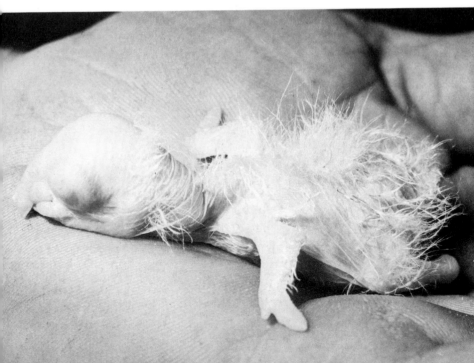

*Hawk-headed Parrot at 17 days. The eyes are starting to open; the ear is still closed.*

*Hawk-headed Parrot at 30 days.*

After the formula is prepared, it is put into small plastic containers and placed in a refrigerator or freezer. A container is removed from the freezer some hours before it is required. Thinning with water may be necessary before use, to produce consistency a little thicker than cream soup. It is stirred well before use and fed at a temperature of 37.7 to 38.3°C (100 to 101°F).

## GRIT

A question which is often asked is whether it is necessary to give grit to seedeating parrots while they are being hand-reared. Species which normally consume much grit, such as Cockatiels, can be given a little fine grit with the food twice weekly, after they are about three weeks old, as some birds do feed grit to their chicks. I have never given grit to the larger, omnivorous parrots.

# 6

# WHEN CHICKS
# ARE ILL

Aviculturists can be transported from the heights of happiness to the depths of despair in a very short time. This is especially true where chicks are the source of pride and joy; for one day they may appear as the picture of health and the next they may be very ill indeed. Deterioration is extremely rapid in sick birds, especially small ones, and when one is ill there is no time to lose.

The experienced and observant breeder will be alerted to the fact that all is not well with a chick early enough to rectify matters, if this is possible. He or she will be ever on the look-out for some small change in behaviour or appearance which may signal the start of ill health.

## WEIGHT

Daily weighing provides an early-warning system which is invaluable and either alerts one to the fact that something is wrong or confirms suspicions that might otherwise be attributed to over-anxiety.

Keeping records of the weight of each chick daily is therefore important. If there are several young which could be difficult to identify individually, they should be marked with nail varnish or felt-tipped pen if too young to ring, then, at a few days old, ringed (banded) with split or closed rings. (These are obtained from ring manufacturers, as very few shops stock them.) Closed rings must be placed on the chick's leg at a very early age, before their eyes open. Split rings can be used at any time (but adult birds of strong-billed species can easily remove those made of plastic). The legs of young birds which have been ringed should be examined regularly as they mature. The leg size of individuals varies; the ring could become embedded in the flesh of large youngsters and, unless noticed in time, could result in a leg being lost in a very painful manner.

A good method of weighing chicks is to use a gram-scale of the spring-balance type; it gives a reasonably accurate reading. These scales

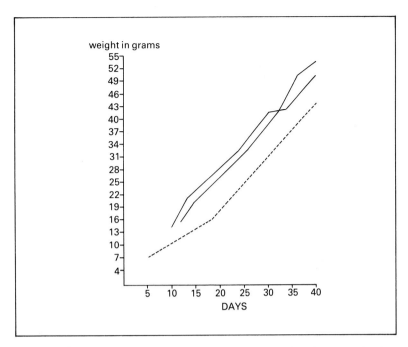

*Fig. 6   Weight gains in hand-reared (-----) and parent-reared (——) Goldie's Lorikeets (*Trichoglossus goldiei*).*

are often used by wild-bird ringers and, in the UK, can be obtained from the British Trust for Ornithology, Beech Grove, Station Road, Tring, Hertfordshire, UK. It is wise to invest in two gram-scales: one which weighs up to 100 g and one which weighs up to 500 g as the gradations on the latter are not fine enough for very small chicks. For scientific work that requires great precision, an instrument such as a Salter Electroscale, which weighs to three decimal places of a gram, is ideal. Such electronic equipment is, of course, very expensive. A machine that weighs to the nearest gram can be obtained for a very great deal less, and is available in most household stores.

When a gram-scale is used chicks should be placed in a small bag such as the plastic type used for groceries or, in the case of tiny chicks, a bag made from a soft paper tissue with adhesive tape. The bag should be discarded after a short period of use. It should be weighed and the weight subtracted from the total to give the chick's weight. Kitchen scales with gram markings can be used for chicks of large species.

All young should be weighed at the same time daily, with the crop empty, preferably before the first feed each morning. Weights can be recorded on a wall calendar hung near the chicks, or in a notebook. A

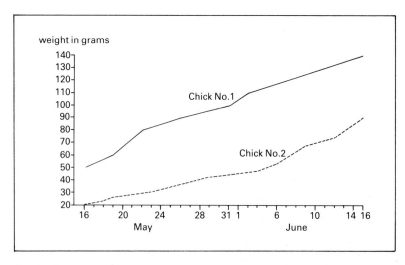

*Fig. 7   Discrepancy in weight of siblings. This is often pronounced, in hand-reared as well as in parent-reared young. The graph shows the growth rate of two Dusky Lory (Pseudeos fuscata) chicks hatched during the last week in April. The development of No. 2 (only two days younger than No. 1) was retarded due to early neglect by the parents.*

steady weight increase should be apparent. This may be very small for the first few days for incubator-hatched chicks and others which have never been fed by their parents. After about two weeks weight gains are generally greater.

Weighing provides a safeguard against failure to notice a chick which is not developing normally. If a chick fails to gain weight for a period well before the weaning stage, or is gaining less weight than its siblings, this is a clear indication that something is wrong. It might be necessary to consult a veterinarian (see page 72).

As chicks approach weaning age and become more active, some are impossible to weigh on a gram-scale or kitchen scale because they refuse to keep still long enough for an accurate reading to be obtained. At this period weight losses will occur. Chicks generally reach a peak in weight some days before weaning.

Too few aviculturists keep records of chick weights. This is regrettable because such information is invaluable to other breeders, especially those rearing a species for the first time, who may be uncertain whether weight gains are normal for the species. All aviculturists are urged to publish such data, preferably in the form of a graph.

As already mentioned, incubator-hatched chicks and those hand-fed from a very early age initially show smaller weight gains that those which are parent-reared. However, by the time weaning age is attained, the

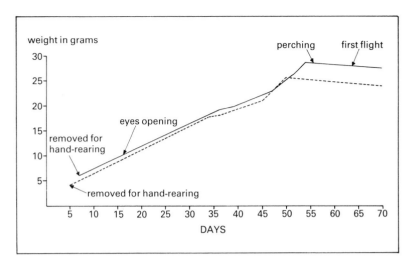

*Fig. 8   Development of sibling chicks (believed male and female) of Tahiti Blue Lory (Vini peruviana). Hatched 18 February 1984 (——) and 20 February 1984 (-----).*

weights will be the same. These differences are most noticeable if only some chicks from one nest are removed for hand-rearing, and parent-reared young are available for comparison. This is regardless of the food fed and would appear to indicate that the parents pass on something beneficial, perhaps bacteria which aid digestion, which cannot be precisely duplicated in manufactured foods.

## SKIN COLOUR

An equally important indicator of health to that of weight is skin colour. This is a pinkish-flesh colour in healthy chicks. A change signals a severe problem. The skin could show a yellowish or dark red tone. The latter often occurs before death. Usually by the time the skin colour changes the chick is dying. Another symptom of sickness is a lowering of the body temperature, in which case extra heat will normally be required immediately.

## FAECES

The faeces do provide some indication of health, in that a change in their appearance or consistency, without a change in the food, usually indicates that something is wrong. If the faeces are tinged with blood or abnormally dark, the problem is a serious one. It is impossible to describe normal faeces in a chick as this depends entirely on the food given and on the species. In the larger parrots chicks have dark droppings, well formed, while in lories, of course, the excreta is more liquid.

## CROP COMPACTION

The most readily-observed sign of ill health is failure of the crop to empty. The moment that every hand-feeder dreads is taking a chick out of the brooder to find that its crop is compacted. With luck, this may never happen, but if it does action must be immediate.

One of the most common causes is offering food which is too thick. I will repeat the advice to err on the side of a thin mixture, if in doubt. Food containing large pieces, such as sunflower kernels, could also be to blame. Over-feeding can result in the same problem, which is why one should never feed a chick until its crop is flat and empty. An early sign of illness or disease is the crop taking longer than usual to empty and, if the chick is fed at the appointed hour without the feeder checking the crop, this sign will pass unnoticed.

One cause which is simply rectified is the temperature in the brooder being too low.

Another cause can be guarded against. Chicks of certain species, such as macaws, have a tendency to pick up pieces of nest litter. One breeder lost seven Eclectus chicks before he had one post-mortemed and discovered that its crop was compacted with wood shavings. Another breeder, hand-rearing his first chick, also an Eclectus, felt the crop when the food ceased to pass through: he realised the reason. As an ex-nurse he had the skill and courage to do something few others would have risked. He inserted long-handled forceps down the throat and into the crop and was able to extract four pieces of wood shavings, one very large. That day only water with milk of magnesia and glucose was given and the following day well diluted food only. The Eclectus later made up its weight loss and grew into a healthy young bird.

I have never experienced this problem with Eclectus or other large parrots because, even before they reach the stage of picking up and swallowing items, a welded mesh base is placed in the brooder. This also provides good exercise for the feet. Alternatively, for large species, you can sift the shavings through a small-mesh wire netting to remove any pieces large enough to swallow.

The final and most alarming cause of failure of the crop to empty is disease. By the time this occurs it may be too late to save the chick. If, for example, there is a growth of the fungus *Candida albicans* in the crop, it may be too well advanced to cure. Or it may be that the kidneys have ceased to function due to fatty liver and kidney syndrome. If a fungal or

*A welded-mesh base in the brooder is recommended for older chicks, such as this Hyacinthine Macaw (*Anodorhynchus hyacinthinus*), hand-reared at Birdworld in England.*

bacterial infection is suspected, a veterinarian should be sought at once, preferably one who has previously treated parrot chicks.

In cases where the crop is compacted, a vet can pass a tube attached to a syringe down the throat and into the crop and, without great difficulty if the food is runny, withdraw the contents. The success of this operation may depend on the availability of the correct size of tube. It is not an especially difficult operation on a large chick but may be impossible on a very small one.

Anyone who has hand-reared parrot chicks over a period of years will have known many traumatic moments. One such instance remains very firmly in my mind. It concerns a Queen of Bavaria's or Golden Conure

(*Aratinga guarouba*) which a friend asked me to rear. This chick was the most aware and intelligent I had ever reared (other breeders have commented on the unusual intelligence of this species). From an early age, while in the brooder, he would watch my movements, peering over the top of his box; and he was especially lovable.

When the young Conure was about five weeks old his crop became compacted due to incorrect food, but the usual methods failed to clear it. The day after the problem occurred there was no improvement; he looked well but constantly called to be fed. I did not have a syringe suitable for removing the crop contents, so in the afternoon I took him along to my veterinarian's surgery. The vet had never previously emptied a chick's crop, but within about one minute of him finding a suitable syringe this had been accomplished. He then washed out the crop with warm water.

For the next few days the food fed was more liquid than normal and the problem did not recur. 'Q' grew into a beautiful bird – and he was such a joy. You have to rear this species to know how appealing it is!

I digressed here to stress how important the co-operation of a good vet can be. Most have little opportunity to work with birds and some welcome the opportunity to gain experience in a neglected field.

One vet treats crop compaction by passing 2.5 ml of warm saline solution into the crop and massaging gently. If a vet is not available, warm saline solution can be given by syringe or spoon. The crop is then massaged gently, and often this has the desired result after a couple of hours. Sometimes the crop is very slow to empty. In this case blackstrap molasses dissolved in hot water can be given every couple of hours and the massage repeated. The fluid prevents dehydration; it does not matter that no food is given.

The chick should be placed on paper towels so that you can see when faeces appear. When they do, the paper should be changed again so that the frequency of defecation is known. Remember that a chick can survive for two or three days, or perhaps more in a large species, on molasses and water. If food is given before the crop has been properly cleared, however, it may result in death, if the contents of the crop become sour and cannot be removed.

If food stays in the crop for a long time, whatever the cause, the contents of the crop become acidic. Some breeders deal with this problem by giving a solution of baking soda or bicarbonate of soda, in order to neutralise the acid.

There is another method of emptying a chick's crop which has been used with success by experienced breeders. I have never used it myself and would not recommend it unless there is positively no alternative. After giving molasses and water and massaging the crop, the thumb and index finger are used to force the crop contents up into the mouth. It may be necessary to hold the chick's head down, and it must be done very quickly or there is a danger that the chick will choke and die.

It may be necessary to resort to surgery if the crop is compacted with hard material, such as the kernels of sunflower seed. This sounds drastic, but there is probably less risk, if carried out competently, than with the previous method. It is quite easy to make an incision between the blood vessels on the skin covering a chick's crop so that very little loss of blood occurs. A veterinarian can do this and stitch the crop after the contents have been removed.

## FUNCTIONAL BLOCKAGE

A possible cause of food remaining in the crop is a functional blockage. For a reason which may not be established, there is a temporary failure of the bowels. This will be evident when no faeces are passed and, in young chicks, the blockage can be detected by the accumulation of faeces seen through the skin near the vent. A veterinarian can relieve the condition by introducing a small length of plastic tubing into the vent, preferably the type used, for example, for dealing with bladder conditions in dogs. It has a closed rounded end with two holes near the end. The faeces can be drawn off using this. If a vet is not available, a very small, warmed thermometer, lubricated with lubricant jelly or even washing-up liquid, can be carefully introduced into the vent, thereby enabling the faeces to be passed, in less severe cases. Liquid only should be given until the chick's condition has returned to normal – if it does. Usually, if the bowel ceases to function, the chick will die.

## FATTY LIVER AND KIDNEY SYNDROME

Another reason for the crop not emptying is kidney failure. Unfortunately, fatty liver and kidney syndrome is a very common cause of death in parrot chicks. Most breeders do not realise this because they do not have post-mortem examinations carried out on chicks.

Fatty liver and kidney syndrome in poultry is believed to be the result of a complex interaction of dietary and environmental factors – and such is probably also the case with parrot chicks. Coutts (1981) states: 'It has been shown that wheat-based diets containing low fat and protein levels tend to give rise to the condition and the energy to protein ratio is also important. How these nutritional factors cause the condition is not understood fully, but recently it has been found that an important role is played by the vitamin biotin.' Since biotin has been added to poultry rations, few cases occur, except where pelleted food has been offered, because biotin may be destroyed by the heat used in the preparation of pellets.

Birds suffering from fatty liver and kidney syndrome show no symptoms until the crop ceases to empty properly. After death there is rapid degeneration and disintegration. Post-mortem examination shows pallor and swelling of the liver and kidneys; both organs are soft. These changes are due to fatty infiltration which also occurs in other organs, including the heart and intestinal tract.

In poultry it has been found that adding molasses to the drinking water has a beneficial effect – and this is believed to be because of its high biotin content. Coincidentally, I had always given molasses dissolved in hot water to parrot chicks whose crops failed to empty properly, years before I knew that fatty liver and kidney syndrome was often the cause and that biotin was beneficial.

Biotin is one of the B-complex vitamins, widely distributed in animals and plants. Good natural sources are liver, kidney, yeast, egg yolk, milk, peas and cereals. Small amounts occur in many vegetables and fruits.

It is known that there is a basic protein in egg white called avidin which combines with biotin and prevents it being utilised by the body. Therefore, the raw white of egg should not be given to chicks. Avidin and biotin form a complex which cannot be broken down by the digestive processes, only by cooking and by irradiation.

In humans a substantial amount of the daily intake of biotin is supplied from synthesis in the intestines by bacteria. Presumably the same occurs in birds. This important source of biotin is reduced greatly if antibiotics are given, thus it would be a wise precaution to supplement the biotin intake of any chick which receives antibiotics.

According to Mervyn (1984) laboratory animals deprived of biotin lost their fur, suffered from an itchy dermatitis, retarded growth and spastic gait. They were susceptible to heart and lung ailments. Puppies fed on a diet lacking in biotin suffered from progressive paralysis. Biotin is considered by some researchers to activate lysozyme, the bacteria digesting anti-enzyme found in body fluids. It may therefore be that this vitamin is very important for a number of aspects of health in parrot chicks.

In poultry chicks signs of biotin deficiency include slow growth, leg problems including slipped tendon, and skin lesions. They consist of thickening of the skin on the underside of the feet with eventual cracking, fissuring and haemorrhaging. Skin lesions heal relatively quickly when adequate levels of biotin are made available; but leg deformities may improve but not be totally rectified.

Multi-vitamin preparations given to birds contain some biotin. For example, Nekton-Bio (Nekton-Produkte, Pforzheim, West Germany) contains 200 mg per 1000 g. Professor Taylor advised me that he felt it was preferable to give biotin in this form, rather than in the pure form in which it is impossible to ration. Large intakes by human babies (10 mg per day) have not proved toxic; the result of excess biotin in birds is unknown. It is possible to obtain biotin tablets from health food stores. Each tablet contains 500 mcg of biotin and the recommended dose for humans is one or two tablets per day.

Another B-complex vitamin, choline, may also play a part in preventing fatty liver and kidney syndrome. In 1939 it was shown that fatty liver could be remedied by giving choline to sufferers. Liver normally contains only 5–7 per cent of its weight in fat, but in the absence of choline the proportion can increase to as much as 50 per cent. Excessive fatty deposits adversely affect the function of this vital organ. Choline prevents fat accumulating in other vital organs, such as the heart and kidneys, by facilitating the transport of fats within the body. Supplementation of the diet with choline not only prevents abnormal accumulation of fat but actually clears it (Mervyn, 1984).

Choline is present in wheat germ, liver, kidney and eggs. The richest source is lecithin. It also occurs in carrots, peas, spinach, turnips, potatoes, soya beans and brussels sprouts.

The amino acid methionine can be converted by the human body into choline. The latter is always present combined with an acid such as hydrochloric (choline chloride), tartaric or citric in pharmaceutical preparations.

A multi-vitamin preparation containing biotin, choline and methionine would therefore appear to be desirable. However, excessive amounts of vitamins should never be added to the diet, especially to those containing human baby foods which are already fortified with vitamins. The British veterinarian George A. Smith has post-mortemed parrot chicks in which the kidneys have been calcified due to an excess of vitamins and minerals.

## FUNGAL INFECTIONS

It has already been mentioned that disease can result in the crop failing to empty. An infection could be the cause; and one of the most common in parrot chicks is that of the fungus *Candida albicans*. It can develop in the mouth, perhaps on the site of an injury, or can grow unseen in the crop (causing persistent vomiting in the later, incurable stage) or other areas.

If its existence is recognised at an early stage it is easy to treat. For this reason every chick's mouth, the interior and the exterior part near the mandibles, should be examined daily. Chicks should be fed in good light, preferably under an angle-poise lamp, so that any abnormality is easily recognised. A wise precaution in chicks of the larger species is to swab the mouth after each feed with a cotton bud, so that bacteria or fungi cannot grow on food adhering inside the beak.

Initially, *Candida albicans* can be seen as small white spots. If left untreated whitish lesions appear. A veterinarian should be consulted immediately for suitable anti-fungal treatment such as Nystan (Nystatin) ointment (E. R. Squibb & Sons Ltd, Hounslow, UK) which can be applied to affected parts or suspension given orally. Another product, Daktarin (Janssen Pharmaceutics, Oxford, UK), can be obtained in the form of an orange-flavoured gel and applied to affected areas. Usually only isolated cases will occur, but if present in several birds being reared Nystatin can be given orally as a precautionary measure to unaffected chicks. Those treated with Nystatin, or other anti-fungal products, must have the diet supplemented with Vitamin A.

*Candida* grows with great rapidity and, if untreated, will be very difficult or impossible to cure.

Sometimes the origin of the problem is known. For example, if excessively hot food is given (i.e. above about 44°C, 112°F) a chick's mouth and/or crop will be burned, making the site vulnerable to an infection of *Candida albicans*. This fungus can, of course, also develop in young being reared by their parents. A pair of Dusky Lories in my possession injured the mouth of one chick and Candidiasis developed. The chick had to be removed from its parents' care and after a few days' application of Nystatin cream it was cured.

Fungus infections are a serious cause of loss of chicks, so much so that some breeders use Nystatin as a preventative, regularly giving it in the food from the time chicks hatch. Using this or other anti-fungal agents as a prophylactic is most unwise, because if this is carried out continuously it could result in a strain of birds which are resistant to its use.

One breeder told me that a fungal disease became apparent in many hand-reared young soon after they started to eat seed (dry sunflower). He believed that it originated from the seed. Other breeders will not feed soaked seed because they believe it to be a source of fungi. When seed becomes damp, either because of the atmosphere or because it has been soaked, it can be the source of fungi which have time to develop if the seed is not eaten within a few hours of rinsing after soaking.

I soak most sunflower seed before feeding it, partly to remove the dirt and dust. Any which is not eaten on the day of soaking is discarded and, to my knowledge, I have never had any problems which resulted from its use. In the USA calcium propionate is widely used by breeders who soak seed. They add one third of a teaspoonful to a gallon of water in which the seed is soaked, as this solution kills fungi.

Cleanliness is of the greatest importance in all matters concerning chicks. It is for this reason that those who hand-rear chicks on a large scale keep them in a separate room in which everything can be washed and disinfected with ease. Ideally the walls should be tiled. However, most chicks will share the breeder's kitchen or one of the dwelling rooms in the house. The kitchen is generally the most suitable because of the presence of running water which facilitates good hygiene. A word of warning, however: chicks and adult birds can be killed by the fumes of hydrofluoric acid, which are given off when non-stick pans are over-heated or burned.

Disease can easily be transmitted among chicks by the feeding tool and, in this respect, a spoon is easier to keep clean than a syringe. Whichever feeding instrument is used it should be sterilised, by standing in a disinfectant between feeds. One commonly in use for this purpose in the USA is Nolvasan. Ordinary bleach can be used to sterilise other equipment not connected with feeding. The breeder should wash his or her hands before and after feeding chicks and between different groups of young.

If one chick is infected with a fungus or some other disease special precautions must be taken. Food should be offered from a separate container and with an implement used for no other chick. If the presence of disease is suspected, but not confirmed, the spoon or syringe should be washed after each chick has been fed.

British veterinary surgeon and parrot breeder George A. Smith (1985b) pointed out: 'Cleanliness in hand-rearing is as essential as the quality of food and warmth. It ought to be obvious that it is dangerous to put part-parent reared chicks with incubator-hatched, human-fostered ones. . . . Chicks which have been with their parents ought to be reared entirely separately. This applies particularly to those that are removed from the nest because they are not being well reared or, particularly, when some have died for they are likely to be suffering from a parent-contracted disease.'

## INTESTINAL WORMS

A possible cause of illness in chicks being hand-reared is intestinal worms, usually *Ascaridia*. They can be passed on by the parents when chicks are very young. A Yellow-fronted Amazon (*Amazona ochrocephala ochrocephala*) which became listless and refused food at seven-and-a-half weeks old was seen to have worms in its faeces (Arman and Arman, 1980). A vet administered Nemicide directly into the crop using a syringe and the next day a knot of worms, the longest 1.25 cm (½ in) long was passed. Later a knot of faeces, solid with worms measuring 3.8 cm (1½ in) long by 10 mm (⅜ in) in diameter was passed. The young

Amazon showed immediate signs of recovery and no more worms were ejected. Both parents had been tested for worms prior to the start of incubation, giving negative results.

## CLOSTRIDIAL INFECTIONS

Parrot chicks are susceptible to clostridial infections. Clostridia are spore-forming bacterial organisms, of which several types can cause problems. *Clostridium septicum* causes gangrenous dermatitis, a bacterial infection of subcutaneous tissues and underlying muscles. *Staphylococcus aureus* may also be involved. Both clostridia and staphylococci occur widely in nature (Coutts, 1981). The former can frequently be isolated from a bird's intestinal content and the latter from its skin, and isolation is not in itself indicative of disease. Coutts states: 'It appears that some form of tissue injury must occur for these organisms to be transformed from harmless commensals to the pathogenic state. This tissue injury may be simple physical damage due to high stocking densities or nutritional deficiency, particularly of Vitamin E or Selenium. Tissue damage resulting from these or other causes favours growth of opportunist organisms which may be present.'

In severe cases bubbles of gas can be seen in the subcutaneous tissues, as well as blood-tinged fluid. If the shanks and feet are affected, the skin peels off easily and the foot pad may be ruptured. The skin of the thighs, wings, back and breast may be coloured blue-black, suggestive of severe bruising. Muscular tissues are dark red or almost black and haemorrhagic. Autopsy may reveal that the liver is swollen and discoloured with necrotic foci in its substance.

Severe cases of gangrenous dermatitis in parrot chicks are probably rare. I had a single, extremely distressing experience of this. At the time I was unable to identify it as a clostridia infection and was mystified by the startling and unpleasant symptoms. A friend had asked me to try to hand-rear two *Charmosyna* lorikeet chicks, as those hatched by the parents invariably died at an early age. The two chicks were removed from the nest when very young, perhaps three or four days old. They were hyper-active, as though uncomfortable or in pain. Severe bleeding occurred from their feet, which were minute. Gas bubbles could clearly be seen under the skin. Both chicks died after about three days.

Coutts recommends treatment with Sulphaquinoxaline in preference to antibiotics such as tetracyclines and penicillin, although these may be effective. Birds in advanced stages of the disease are not likely to respond to treatment, however. Disinfection with iodine-based disinfectant should be carried out following an outbreak.

It may be necessary to treat chicks with antibiotics. If so, use them with caution and only on veterinary advice. I have used Synulox palatable drops (clavulanate-potentiated amoxycillin) (Beecham Animal Health, Brentford, Middlesex, UK) and found them to be harmless and effective.

## FOOT DEFORMITIES

Finally, there is a different kind of problem which, though not fatal, can result in chicks being incapacitated for life: foot deformities. Sometimes these occur despite the best precautions, but every care should be taken to avoid them.

The most usual reasons are as follows.

1) *Incorrect diet*, i.e. vitamin or mineral deficiency. The importance of giving biotin has already been mentioned (see page 63); foot deformities can also result from a deficiency. Rickets is one of the commonest forms of foot deformities, caused by a deficiency of vitamin D if calcium is present in the diet, or of both substances. Without vitamin D the calcium cannot be absorbed and the bones will be brittle and easily broken. Rickets is easily prevented by adding Collo-Cal D to the rearing food (a calcium and vitamin $D_3$ supplement which can be obtained from any vet). Rickets may also be due to an imbalance of calcium and phosphorus or to a phosphorus deficiency.

Manganese deficiency is the cause of the condition known as perosis or slipped tendon (Coutts, 1981). The hock joints become enlarged and distorted and the lower end of the tibia may become bent or bowed, resulting in the slipping of the Achilles (or gastrocnemius) tendon from its normal position on the rear of the hock.

It should be noted that absorption of manganese from the intestine can be reduced by high levels of calcium and phosphorus in the food. Giving large amounts of calcium to prevent rickets could therefore have the reverse effect to that desired. Slipped tendon is not necessarily due to manganese deficiency but could be caused by lack of choline and biotin or due to genetic influences.

Advanced cases of leg deformities resulting from dietary deficiency are not usually curable.

2) *Slippery surfaces*. Chicks kept on surfaces which do not offer a good grip, such as soft paper tissues, after they are four or five days old, are liable to suffer from splayed legs. Up to this age the container should be small or the chicks nestled into the middle of it by packing material around them. At feeding times they should be placed on a towel or other surface affording a good grip.

3) *Congenital defects*. This cause would be rare and difficult to prove but

*At 55 days old this Duivenbode's Lory* (Chalcopsitta duivenbodei) *had three toes on one foot pointing forward. By then it was too late to correct this fault.*

should be suspected if a pair consistently produces young with deformed feet.

What can be done to cure foot deformities? In some cases no cure is possible. In others, one of the following measures may succeed.

a) If noticed at an early age, the legs can be splinted to attempt straightening. Splints should be changed every three to five days.

b) Fit a closed ring on one leg of the affected chick and a split ring on the other leg. Wire the two rings together (plastic bag binder wire is useful) so that the legs are the normal distance apart. Leave for three weeks. Alternatively, taping the legs can be tried, or the use of a bandage tied in the shape of a figure of eight. However, tape and bandage cause stress to most chicks, especially as it is difficult to use them in a way which permits the chick to walk around. In some parrot chicks one of the back toes points forward. Correction should be attempted as soon as it is noticed, otherwise the condition will be permanent. Later in life this can result in the toenail growing into the toe, so every effort should be made to correct it at an early age. Taping the toe into the correct position usually succeeds with young chicks. It should be realised, however, that in some species it is not unusual for three toes to point forward at an early age and this is invariably corrected as the chick grows. Only experience enables one to distinguish between what is normal and abnormal in this respect.

c) Placing a chick on welded mesh as soon as a deformity is noticed may help. A false base of welded mesh in the brooder is, in any case, desirable from the age of a few days, to prevent them ingesting nest litter.

d) One breeder found 'Blu-tack', a re-usable adhesive, invaluable for rectifying foot deformities. This plasticine-like substance is easily moulded to the required shape.

*An Umbrella Cockatoo (*Cacatua alba*) aged 45 days. The clenched feet are typical of many cockatoos at this stage – they are not a sign of deformity.*

Chicks are kept on soft paper tissues until they are just over a week old. On several occasions, however, bleeding from minute cuts on the feet has occurred. I suspect that the tissues may be to blame; possibly they contain a chemical which adversely affects the delicate feet of tiny chicks. If such bleeding occurs, the feet should be treated with an antibiotic powder and the nest lining changed immediately to a different surface.

A problem that requires immediate action is swollen toes. If untreated the blood supply to the toes will not be maintained, and the whole toe or part of it will be lost. An antibiotic, prescribed by a veterinarian, will probably be effective if given as soon as the swelling occurs. Again, I suspect the infection may originate from the surface on which the chick is kept, but it does occur also in parent-reared young.

It is advisable to consult a veterinary surgeon as soon as any foot abnormality is noticed. Although a vet may have little experience with birds, he can often apply knowledge gained with other animals to avian problems. Never give up hope in very young chicks: the condition may improve. As an example, a Dusky Lory (*Pseudeos fuscata*) which I removed from the nest was found on X-ray to have a greenstick fracture (one which occurs when the bones are still soft) of the left leg. It was held at right-angles to the body. There seemed little hope that it would be normal, so it was kept on welded mesh, forcing it to use its legs at a very early age. By the time it was old enough to perch, it could do so normally, its oddly-set leg being apparent only when it ran on a flat surface.

The loss of chicks, especially those that are feathered, is a very upsetting experience, but one that every hand-rearer will suffer sooner or later. However, many losses could be prevented; chicks die needlessly because the breeder is slow to take action or seek advice. Remember that speed is of paramount importance when dealing with an ailing chick and, at the first suspicion that something is wrong, steps should be taken to rectify matters. Often valuable time is lost searching for someone who can help. Before you take your first chick from the nest make a point of finding someone you can turn to who can advise you, and of seeking a vet in your area who is interested in birds.

One thing that he can do, regardless of experience, is to take a sample of the chick's droppings. These will be sent to a laboratory and a sensitivity test carried out to discover if the condition will respond to antibiotics, and if so, which ones. It is a few days before the outcome of such tests are known – yet another reason for acting with great speed.

Comparatively little is known about the diseases of parrots and their young so do not expect all the answers to be readily available. You may encounter a problem concerning which the most experienced hand-rearer or veterinarian is unable to be of any practical help.

# 7

# WEANING – PATIENCE IS THE KEYWORD

Of all matters concerned with the hand-rearing of parrots, it is the weaning process in which the individuality of chicks is most apparent. It would therefore be unwise to lay down any hard-and-fast rules regarding this most important period in the life of a young bird.

Hand-fed parrots can often be weaned at an earlier age than those left with their parents. This can be encouraged by offering soft items of food at which they can nibble well before they are actually capable of eating them. As most chicks nibble at everything with which they come into contact, there is no problem in persuading them to sample such foods.

In my experience sweetcorn, soft pear, soaked sunflower seed and spray millet are the items which are preferred initially. Of course, much depends on the species and the individual. There is no harm in offering such foods too early and finding that they are ignored, but weaning may be difficult if you wait until a chick becomes awkward to feed. If they are fed sunflower kernels in the mixture, as they approach weaning age the sunflower should be ground less finely so that they can feel the small pieces in the mouth. The feeder should pause between each spoonful and the chicks will chew up the larger particles.

## WEANING AGE

As the length of time which a parrot spends in the nest depends primarily on the species, one cannot generalise regarding the age at which young should be weaned. It is important to know at what age the species concerned normally leaves the nest when parent-reared. You can expect a hand-reared chick to show some interest in sampling food a week or so before this. Lories are an exception and, as they take mainly liquid food, may do so long before the normal fledging period. I have had Black-capped Lories (*Lorius lory*), which normally leave the nest at about ten weeks, independent at eight weeks. However, although they readily took warm food and then warm nectar, it was not until they were about 12 weeks old that they would take cold food.

As an approximate guide only, weaning dates are given in the table below. These are based on hand-reared chicks. It must be remembered that individuals of the same species, and even in the same nest, can vary greatly in the age at which they become independent.

| Species | Parent-reared | Hand-reared | |
|---|---|---|---|
| | Young leave nest | Start to feed | Independent |
| Duivenbode's Lory* | 11 weeks | 7 weeks | 11 weeks |
| (Chalcopsitta duivenbodei) | | | |
| Goldie's Lorikeet* | 60–63 days | 38 days | 59–63 days |
| (Trichoglossus goldiei) | | | |
| Meyer's Lorikeet* | 7½ weeks | 6 weeks | 67 days |
| (Trichoglossus flavoviridis meyeri) | | | |
| Roseate Cockatoo* | 8 weeks | 5–6 weeks | 8 weeks |
| (Cacatua roseicapilla) | | | |
| Lesser (Timor) | about 11 weeks | 7 weeks | 12 weeks |
| Sulphur-crested Cockatoo* | | | |
| (Cacatua sulphurea parvula) | | | |
| Moluccan Cockatoo | 13–15 weeks | about 12 weeks | 15 weeks |
| (Cacatua moluccensis) | | | |
| White-tailed Black Cockatoo | 11½ weeks | — | 8½ months |
| (Calyptorhynchus funereus baudini) | | | |
| Blue and Yellow Macaw | about 12 weeks | 10 weeks | 13–20 weeks |
| (Ara ararauna) | | | |
| Scarlet Macaw | 11–12 weeks | 10–11 weeks | 4 months |
| (Ara macao) | | | |
| Brotogeris parrakeets | 6 weeks | 6–7 weeks | 9 weeks |
| Yellow-billed Amazon | 9 weeks | 8 weeks | 11 weeks |
| (Amazona collaria) | | | |
| Yellow-shouldered Amazon* | 9 weeks | 8 weeks | 11½ weeks |
| (Amazona barbadensis) | | | |
| Grey Parrot* | 12 weeks | 8 weeks | 12 weeks |
| (Psittacus erithacus) | | | |
| Eclectus Parrot* | 11 weeks | 9 weeks | 12–14 weeks |
| (Eclectus roratus) | | | |
| Pesquet's Parrot | about 12 weeks | 62 days | 14 weeks minimum |
| (Psittrichas fulgidus) | | | |

*Hand-reared by the author

If in doubt about the age at which a species would normally be weaned, try to seek the advice of a breeder of that particular species. Unfortunately, totally misleading and incorrect advice has been offered by those with no experience of hand-rearing. In one American book a table of 'comparative nesting periods' makes sweeping and dangerous generalisations. For example, the 'age at independence' for lories and lorikeets is given as eight to nine weeks and cockatoos as thirteen to fourteen weeks. With the exception of the small Australian lorikeets which are unknown in aviculture outside Australia (and are not common there), as well as Goldie's, no lorikeet is independent at eight weeks. The larger species are weaned at about thirteen weeks and most of the small ones at approximately ten weeks.

As for cockatoos, the development of various species has greater extremes than in any other group of parrots. The Roseate Cockatoo or Galah is exceptional for its short fledging period; parent-reared young spend at most eight weeks in the nest. Of three which I hand-reared, two were independent at eight weeks and the third (youngest) at nine weeks. In contrast, the Black Cockatoos (*Calyptorhynchus*) have a longer weaning period than any other parrot; indeed, young will be fed by their parents for as long as twelve months, until the pair nest again. Hand-reared young can be weaned as early as eight or nine months.

The Roseate Cockatoos mentioned above were removed for hand-rearing because the parents had hatched six young – an exceptional number. Three were left with the parents and the eldest chick left the nest at about eight weeks old. On the following day, the eldest of the three hand-reared young flew for the first time, aged seven weeks; thus development of those removed from the nest was, perhaps, slightly more advanced. These particular youngsters started to chew up the kernels of

*Fig. 9   Rate of growth of three Roseate Cockatoo (*Cacatua roseicapilla*) chicks hatched during the last week in May. The growth curve of No. 2 shows perhaps the most typical reduction in weight at weaning. No. 3 was not weaned when the graph was completed, for it became impossible to weigh them after 19 July.*

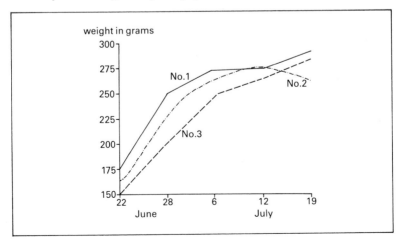

75

sunflower seed when aged between five and six weeks. They were weaned onto soaked sunflower seed and millet sprays, spinach, lettuce, sweetcorn, carrot and peas in the pod.

## INDICATIONS OF READINESS FOR WEANING

There are several indications that young birds are approaching the age at which they will commence to feed themselves. They become more difficult to feed and some would rather play with the spoon, or attempt to upset the food, or flap their wings when removed from the brooder. These are signs that the chick would attempt to feed itself if allowed to. This behaviour will also be observed during the period when the chick starts to feed itself. Another indication is that the chick ceases to gain weight. During this period, chicks from one clutch should be fed in rotation, rather than removing them all from the brooder. Placing them together near the food results in a chaotic free-for-all with each chick jostling to reach the spoon.

It is at this stage that a chick's individuality really asserts itself. Some young parrots are very obstinate and refuse to be fed, or to take more than one or two spoonfuls, when they start to feed on their own; others will always accept spoon-feeding, even when totally independent. Two Goffin's Cockatoos (*Cacatua goffini*) which I reared, which were six

*Some breeders keep chicks, such as these Queen of Bavaria's Conures (*Aratinga guarouba*), in large plastic bowls, when they are feathered.*

months old and had long ceased to need to be fed, were allowed their liberty in the room for a short period each day (Low, 1980b). They would line up to be fed with other chicks being hand-reared at the time!

Then there is the other extreme. Some chicks insist on weaning themselves very early and with extreme rapidity. There is no way that one can feed them, since when offered the spoon they close their beaks quite firmly and literally run away. Fortunately, this behaviour is normally seen only in chicks which are feeding themselves so well that spoon-feeding is no longer necessary, even though it may have been only two weeks since they started to feed on their own.

## WEANING METHOD

Where possible, weaning should be a gradual process. Sometimes it is preferable to reduce the amount of food given at each feed, rather than reduce the number of feeds. This is because giving a smaller quantity of food than the chick is used to receiving stimulates it to start feeding itself. Only when it is taking an appreciable amount of food should the number of feeds per day be reduced, to four, then three, then morning and evening, then evening only. Even when young birds are feeding well on their own I like to give them a late evening feed, to ensure that they roost with full crops.

When food is first offered it should be placed on the floor of the cage, or in a small spill-proof container on the floor. The larger parrots often prefer soaked sunflower seed to start with, and very quickly learn how to remove the husks. It is not necessary to buy shelled sunflower from health food shops. Spray millet is another favourite item; the seeds will be removed before the young bird is capable of eating them, but this is all good practice. One Goffin's Cockatoo started to remove such seeds when six weeks old and to crack sunflower seed at seven weeks. This species normally spends about ten weeks in the nest. This chick was one of the most difficult I have reared in that from the age of three weeks it became reluctant to feed. It ceased to respond to the spoon with the normal head-pumping movement which makes most young psittacines so easy to feed. The only course of action was to make the food even more liquid than normal and literally pour it down the chick's throat. Before it was six weeks old it would start to masticate any small lumps in the mixture, thus I knew it was time to give it some seed to nibble. Its upbringing required a great deal of patience; indeed, patience is the keyword in weaning parrots. Never be in a hurry to have them off your hands.

A wide variety of items can be offered to chicks as they start to pick up food. They would appear to be attracted by the texture, as well as by the taste, and perhaps by the colour. Warm cooked peas are often a favourite. In addition to seed and fruit, such foods as breakfast cereals and digestive biscuits can be offered. Robin Pickering of Co. Durham, who is very successful in hand-rearing Scarlet Macaws (*Ara macao*), told me that the first food they sample is digestive biscuit. At first they crumble them up; although very little is eaten, such foods encourage young birds to start to feed on their own.

In the UK John Stoodley pioneered the idea of giving soaked beans and pulses to parrots. Such beans as mung, haricot and field can be soaked overnight, then minced in a blender and offered with sweetcorn, to add variety to the diet of chicks starting to pick up food. They can also be cooked and minced and added to the rearing food, as can soya beans.

Lories are the easiest of all parrot chicks to wean. They will lap liquid food long before they are fully feathered. The most exceptional case in my experience was a Dusky Lory (*Pseudeos fuscata*) which, when offered nectar at 41 days, drank ravenously and never again allowed itself to be fed. This species normally spends about 11 weeks in the nest. It is the only example I have ever known of instant weaning! Some lories will eat soft pear as early as five weeks, and will drink nectar soon after, due to their habit of testing everything with the tongue. However, hand-feeding must be continued for three to eight weeks longer, depending on the species. Nectar can be mixed in with the rearing food, until they accept nectar on its own, or one can offer nectar and rearing food in separate containers. Usually they show a preference for nectar by the time they are weaned. This should be warmed until they reach the age of weaning.

Normally no problems are experienced with single chicks of lories or other species, which start to feed just as readily as those reared with others. If one should be slow to learn, it will help to place it with or near a young bird which is independent.

Ramon Noegel (1985) related the story of a Hyacinthine Macaw which, at five months, was still being fed twice a day and showed no inclination to feed itself. It was therefore placed in an enclosure with an adult but trustworthy Blue and Yellow Macaw. He wrote: 'The secret to weaning became obvious: competition was the key.' It monopolised the food container to keep the other macaw away from the food and was thus quickly weaned. At only ten weeks it had started to pick up soaked monkey chow and dog chow, also seedless grapes, when kept with a Hawk-headed Parrot chick of the same age. However, competition can lead to young birds consuming an excessive amount of food, so it should be limited. Subsequently, Hyacinthine Macaws reared by Ramon Noegel were weaned as early as three months of age.

The type of food on which a chick has been reared, also the implement with which it has been fed, may have some influence on the weaning process. I suspect that spoon-fed young may be easier to wean than those which are syringe-fed. George Smith has suggested that chicks fed on cereal-based baby foods and milk, but not ground up seed, will take up seed, husk it but not swallow it. Although they visually recognise seed as food this is not corroborated by their experience of taste, thus they discard it. Therefore coarsely ground sunflower kernels, also fruit juices, should be included in the food of young birds approaching weaning. It is no longer necessary to provide hot food; warm food is accepted or even preferred.

At this stage their temperament can alter. Some bite out of mischief, not malice. They should be corrected with a tap on the beak and a firm 'No!' They soon learn that it is wrong – but this does not necessarily prevent a sly nip on the ear or neck! You must try very hard never to lose your patience; this could result in them biting hard and becoming difficult to feed and handle, and possibly even completely spoiling their temperament so that they are unsuitable for pets.

The sharpness of the claws of many young parrots at this age can also cause problems. In small species they can be like needles, and in large ones they can penetrate the skin to the degree that they draw blood. I do not agree, however, with cutting the nails of young birds. If necessary, nails can be filed, at the tip only, with a nail file or emery board.

## THE WEANING CAGE

Just as the transition from spoon-feeding to independence should be a gradual one, so, in my opinion should that from brooder to cage and then aviary. When young are fully feathered they can be removed from the brooder to an unheated cage. Examples of ages at which I have transferred chicks are Iris Lorikeet and Duivenbode's Lory, 7 weeks, Yellow-shouldered Amazon, 54 days, and Eclectus Parrot, 9 weeks. I use a wooden box with a hinged lid and a welded mesh front which has been specially made for the purpose. Newspaper is placed below a false floor of welded mesh, thus ensuring the young birds never become fouled by their own excreta. This is the chief reason for not using a parrot cage. However, some on the market which have a plastic base clipped onto the top can be adapted by cutting a piece of welded mesh to fit above the plastic base. Even so, a weaning cage of the type described is to be preferred in my opinion. Being completely enclosed except for the front, it provides a greater feeling of security.

A low perch should be placed in the weaning cage as young birds should be encouraged to perch as soon as possible. The height of the perch is gradually increased. After a couple of weeks the youngsters can be moved to an ordinary parrot cage and, after several more weeks, to an indoor flight, if desired.

*Weaning cage used by the author – a simple wooden box with hinged lid and welded-mesh front and false floor. It offers a greater sense of security than a parrot cage.*

## DIET AFTER WEANING

Because a young parrot is weaned, it does not mean that one can cease to pay attention to its diet. During this period it will try new foods more readily than at any other period in its life. The variety of items offered should therefore be very wide and the amount of seed as small as possible. Seed should not be the most important part of the diet! Offer, for example, sprouted mung beans, for their nutritional properties are far superior to seed. A great favourite with all species is pomegranate – which, regrettably, has a short season of availability.

I continue to provide soaked sunflower seed in preference to dry seed for many weeks and, if the young bird is going to a new home, I suggest that the purchaser does likewise. Soaked seed is easier for a young bird to digest; it is simply soaked in cold water for between 24 and 48 hours and rinsed well under a running tap before feeding. Nearly all parrots will take soaked sunflower in preference to dry; and there is no reason why they should ever be offered dry seed except those kept in outdoor aviaries in freezing weather or very humid climates. Cleanliness of food containers and removal of uneaten seed after 24 hours is most important when soaked seed is fed. However, it is so much cleaner and more palatable that the small effort required to provide it is well worthwhile.


## FLYING

Soon after it starts to feed on its own a young parrot will begin to flap its wings with great vigour. When it discovers that it can fly the novelty of this form of exercise may be so great that when removed for feeding it shows more interest in exercising its wings. If this is the case, let it have a good flap before trying to feed it.

Many young parrots are very strong on the wing and may injure themselves if allowed to take off unsupervised. On no account should they be taken out of doors as a sudden fright could cause them to take off and disappear over the horizon. I know of several instances in which this has happened to unweaned youngsters. In one case a hand-reared Goldie's Lorikeet (*Trichoglossus goldiei*) was at liberty for two days before it made its way back to its parents' aviary, ignoring another pair of the same species in the same range – a truly extraordinary feat.


## TEMPERAMENT

As chicks approach the age of weaning their temperament may change, not only towards the person responsible for them but also towards other chicks, if kept with young of other species. Most young parrots are gentle towards others in the brooder, especially single chicks which seem far more contented when reared with others. I reared a Timor Lesser Sulphur-crested Cockatoo with two female Eclectus Parrots. The latter are not renowned for their good humour; even hand-reared birds are often lacking in affection. However, one of the females was befriended by the Timor Cockatoo and it was amusing to see them preening each other. The cockatoo always sat touching the Eclectus. Physical contact and mutual preening are important to cockatoos, unlike Eclectus, which seldom or never preen each other and almost never perch in actual contact.

Two Dusky Lories (*Pseudeos fuscata*) were reared with three Roseate Cockatoos which were younger than themselves. When the lories were feathered and were removed from the brooder they cried incessantly, apparently missing the warmth of their companions, for when returned they ceased to cry.

Lories and cockatoos are affectionate birds and to be trusted with other chicks. When I hand-reared Cruentata Conures (*Pyrrhura cruentata*) they were lacking in affection towards each other and towards myself. One breeder had a tragic experience with this conure when he housed five-week-old chicks with a Red-capped Parrot (*Pionopsitta pileata*), a quiet and gentle species. The Pyrrhuras attacked it and injured it so badly that it subsequently died. One must therefore always bear in mind the differing temperament of species.

Another factor not to be ignored is that pet parrots kept in the same room as chicks being hand-reared may become very jealous of them. Those allowed their liberty in the room must be watched when chicks are being fed. A pet Amazon in my possession flew down onto the floor when a chick being reared was placed there for a few seconds while the brooder was being cleaned. There was no doubt at all that its intent was to attack the chick. Similar signs of jealousy have been observed in other long-standing pets who definitely resent all the attention given to chicks, or perhaps especially a single chick.

## PLUMAGE

One aspect of looking after young birds at the weaning stage which must not be neglected is care of the plumage. Siblings of some species, such as

*As they mature, the head-pumping movements of chicks being hand-fed become very vigorous, resulting in food being spilled on the plumage. It must be wiped off immediately after feeding. A Roseate Cockatoo (*Cacatua roseicapilla*) at the weaning stage is seen here.*

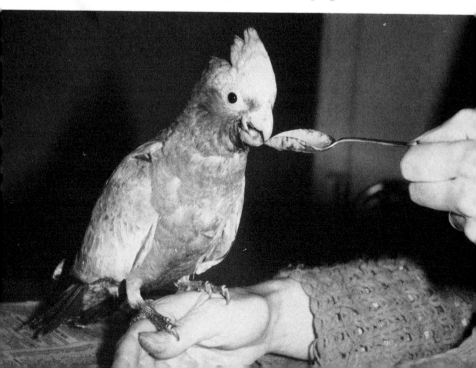

lories, will preen each other and the plumage will be in excellent condition, provided that surplus food is always removed after feeding. However, most young will benefit from being sprayed very lightly with warm water, provided that they are in a warm room and cannot become chilled. Others, notably lories, will bathe at a very early age, soon after becoming independent, thus a shallow dish of water should be available to them.

In my opinion, there is only one aspect of hand-reared birds which does not compare with parent-reared birds – and that is plumage, in certain species. For example, cockatoos which are invariably preened regularly by their parents in the nest emerge with a better 'finish' to the feather than hand-reared young.

Certain youngsters have such a vigorous head-pumping movement when being fed that it is impossible not to spill food around the beak; it may also adhere right under the base of the lower mandible. If this is not removed, the feathers will become matted together. Attempting to remove the dried food is not only difficult but it causes much stress to young at weaning age. It is therefore most important that feathers are cleaned daily, if necessary. A 'bib' of paper towel placed around the neck helps to prevent food being spilled on the plumage. Before a young bird goes to its new home or into an aviary, its plumage must be in perfect condition.

# 8

# INDIVIDUAL
# TREATMENT

Recognising that chicks are individuals and that the needs of those of the same species may vary is very important. It may be the experienced breeder who most needs to be reminded of this fact since he or she may become blasé, especially after a run of trouble-free chicks. The beginner is more likely to watch each chick anxiously and perhaps to search for reasons when something goes wrong. The experienced breeder may accept more easily that there will be a few deaths among chicks being hand-reared and perhaps not bother to question why.

Some deaths could be avoided with the realisation that certain chicks need special treatment and intensive care in their first few days.

A Grey Parrot (*Psittacus erithacus*) which I removed from the egg was one such case. The egg was placed in a Turn-X incubator on November 8; it was believed to have been laid three weeks previously. On November 14, at noon, there was a pip mark, and a second by 2 pm. Humidity within the incubator was increased to 80 per cent. The chick was not heard calling until 4 pm the next day when the third and final pip mark was made.

At 5 pm on November 16, after the chick had been calling strongly for 24 hours, I attempted to release it from the shell. After about one half of the shell had been removed blood was apparent and it was obvious that the attempt to release the chick was premature. No more shell was removed and the chick was placed in a brooder set at about 37° C (99° F). A drop of boiled water and pomegranate juice (for its high iron content, to counteract the loss of blood) was given to the chick occasionally with the aid of a small plastic spoon. This was very difficult because of the foetal position of the chick.

At 9 am the next day the shell was loosened by dipping a small hair paintbrush in hot water and placing it between chick and shell. No attempt was made to remove the shell because the umbilicus was still attached. The chick seemed weaker and its voice was no longer strong. It

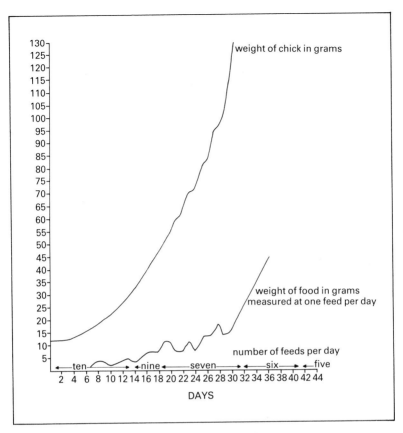

*Fig. 10   Growth and food intake of the Grey Parrot chick.*

was given a drop of the liquid described every couple of hours or so – a very difficult task, because it had little strength. It was not until 5 pm when it made vigorous movements as though hatching that I dared to think it might survive.

At 3 am the next morning it was still in the shell, attached by the umbilical cord which had dried out. I snipped it with small scissors, and puffed Acramide (antibacterial dressing powder, Dale Pharmaceuticals Ltd) on the navel. At 6.30 am it seemed stronger and was calling loudly. Later in the morning the down on the head had dried out; that on the upper part of the body had dried by the afternoon, giving the characteristic fluffy appearance of Grey Parrot chicks.

When the shell was removed it was apparent that part of the yolk sac was unabsorbed. At that time the faeces were fairly solid, dark green and white, which would not have resulted from the very thin liquid the chick was being fed, but from the yolk previously absorbed. Later in the day the faeces were very watery so I started to feed egg yolk and pomegranate juice mixed with boiled water and heated. A normal chick would still have had the benefit of the sustenance from the yolk sac within it. Egg yolk was therefore given to make good this deficiency.

At this stage very minute amounts of food were swallowed, along with much air. There was no feeding response; feeding was stimulated by holding the spoon beneath the tip of the upper mandible. The chick lapped the food but tired very quickly. Only from watching the throat movement was it apparent that food was being swallowed.

I made the mistake of feeding too frequently, every hour approximately, and there was air in the crop most of the time and sometimes the chick was reluctant to feed. I then realised that egg yolk was much more nutritious than the usual thin mixture given to newly-hatched chicks and that such frequent feeding was not necessary. At the 3 am and 6 am feeds the following morning the crop was empty and the chick fed much more readily. It was given a little food at 7.45 am but was not eager to take it. At 9 am it stood up and called very loudly. When fed it took the food well, and I decided not to feed it again until it called for food. However, it slept until 12.20 pm when I awoke it. The crop was empty and again it fed well.

The next day, November 20, was notable for the fact that at last the chick's feeding response was normal – in fact, extremely strong. At 7 pm it grasped the spoon and pumped very strongly. Egg yolk had been discontinued and the food now consisted of a thin mixture of Heinz tinned Pure Fruit, and Bone and Beef Broth with Vegetables, mixed with water.

The temperature in the brooder was maintained at about 33° C (92° F) but if it dropped below this the chick showed no discomfort, as it did if the temperature rose much above this. By the next day, November 21, it was crying much of the time, even although its crop was not empty; possibly the temperature was a little too high for it. Feeding took place every one-and-a-half to two hours during the day until 11.30 pm, then at 3 am, and 6.30 am. The chick had ceased to take in air and feeding had become quick and easy.

The chick continued to thrive and was making weight gains of 1 g per day or more. This was well below that of other Grey chicks which I had reared from the egg, but I was not concerned because the chick was strong and gaining weight steadily. Calculating November 17 as the day of hatching, when the chick weighed 13 g, after six days it weighed 17.5 g, whereas chicks which I had reared previously which had weighed between 12 g and 15 g on hatching weighed 17 g to 23 g on day six (the 17 g chick being one which weighed only 12 g on hatching).

On November 23 the thin membrane attached to the unabsorbed yolk sac, which was like a fine, dry piece of thread, broke; it had dried up days previously and could have been removed. Also on that day, use of the small glass container, 8 cm (3 in) in diameter and 3.5 cm (1½ in) high, used to contain the chick, was discontinued as the droppings were copious enough to make the tissues very wet between feeds. The chick was then nestled in paper tissues in the plastic container lined with paper towel, which had previously held the glass container. All this time a tissue was lightly laid over the chick, as well.

It was still well covered in down and its skin had become a healthy pink; for the first few days it had looked anaemic. The first slit marks were apparent on the eyelids.

From November 29 two or three drops of Collo-Cal D were added to the food on alternate days. A little wheat germ cereal was also added and this slight thickening meant that the feeding frequency could be extended to over two hours as the crop was taking this length of time to empty.

By December 1 the chick was sleeping nearly all the time between feeds and crying rarely. The night feed was extended until 4.30 am. The eyelids were now slit just enough to expose the iris as a narrow dark slit. The ears were still sealed. Significant weight gains, i.e. over 3 g per day, occurred after December 2. On that day the chick's weight jumped from 34.5 g to 40 g, and 7 g of food were taken at the measuring feed, whereas previously the largest amount had been 5 g. The last feed in the early hours of the morning was given on December 5 and from then on the feeding frequency was every three hours during the day, as sometimes there was still food in the crop after 2½ hours.

On December 9 there was a worrying occurrence. The chick's left leg seemed to have lost strength. When the chick was removed for feeding the leg splayed out and the chick fell over on a couple of occasions. The paper towel was removed and replaced by very coarse wood shavings, too large to be ingested. A slight weakness was apparent the next day but thereafter the leg seemed normal. It is of interest that on those two days weight gains totalled only 4 g, whereas on the following and previous days weight gains had been between 5 g and 8 g.

By December 12 the eyes were almost wide open. Feather tracts were apparent all over the body and the wings were darkening with feathers under the skin. A sparse covering of down remained on the upper parts. By then the chick was comfortable at a temperature of 29° C (86° F).

At 29 days, on December 15, the chick's left ear was open and it was making preening movements over non-existent feathers. By this stage its entire body was darkened by second down quills about 4 mm long, visible under the skin and just erupting. Sunflower meal (ground

*The Grey Parrot chick (*Psittacus erithacus*) at 25 days when the diet consisted of the tinned baby foods shown, plus wheat germ cereal and ground sunflower seed.*

sunflower kernels) was added to the food. Two days later the right ear was open. At 32 days old the feeding frequency was every three and a half hours – the length of time which it took for the crop to empty. The food was by then fairly thick, consisting of half a tin each of Heinz Pure Fruit and Bone and Beef Broth with Vegetables, 10 g of ground sunflower kernels, 12 g of wheat germ cereal and about 100 ml of boiled water. This quantity lasted for one day.

By this stage the young Grey was very responsive – standing up in his box and stretching his long neck when called. His feet were light grey. At 38 days the wing feathers were erupting. A week later the body was well covered with very pale grey woolly down. The feet were dark grey and about three-quarters the size of an adult's. In most chicks of this age the feet appear enormous compared with the size of the body. During the day he was free to walk about the brooder on a surface of welded mesh and was replaced in the box lined with coarse shavings at night so that he could rest more comfortably.

He was too active to weigh after 37 days, when a weight of 180 g was recorded. Referring to a graph of other Grey chicks I had hand-reared, I found that the usual weight at this age was between 185 and 190 g.

Rearing of the young Grey progressed uneventfully until the age of 15 weeks. At this stage he was still being fed three times daily but feeding quite well on sweetcorn, the wheat flakes from muesli, soaked sunflower seed and spray millet. On March 2 he was difficult to feed – not unusual for most birds of this age but abnormal for this particular youngster. The next day it was necessary to take him on a car journey of nearly three hours' duration each way. He vomited on the outward journey, but this was believed to be due to the motion of the car. On the homeward journey he again vomited but by then it was apparent that he was ill. He cried often and seemed cold. He spent the night in the heated brooder but next morning was very ill and continuing to vomit. The temperature was increased to about 31°C (88°F). Belatedly I realised that he was dehydrated as a result of not drinking in strange surroundings on the previous day. Honey water with vitamins was given at least every two hours – and no food. He was obviously suffering from sour crop so bicarbonate of soda was given in the honey water and in the drinking water in the brooder. This is to neutralise the acid in the crop.

By evening he was too ill to open his eyes while being fed, yet still took food readily. The antibiotic Synulox (clavulanate-potentiated amoxycillin, Beecham Animal Health, Brentford, Middlesex, UK) was given in the food. He was fed throughout the night. Next morning he seemed slightly better and was vomiting less. Occasionally he went to the water and drank huge quantities. His eyes were still closed most of the time and, although he would respond to the presence of those he knew outside the brooder, his condition seemed to deteriorate again. Either the Synulox was not effective or the dose had been too small. A little weak baby food was given because he was becoming very weak and thin, but most of this was vomited. However, all along some food was going through him and he fed readily.

I was only then able to contact my veterinary surgeon who advised no alteration in the treatment and to give as much fluid as possible. He felt that Synulox should be effective but there had been no improvement later in the day so Framycetin (trade name Framomycin – C-Vet, Bury St Edmunds) was prescribed. The recommended dose is about 250 mg to one pint of water. However, as this antibiotic is not absorbed, for a faster cure a much higher dose can be given for a crop infection, thus Framycetin was given at about 400 times the recommended dose. (It is not injectable, being toxic if given in this way.)

However, he was still vomiting and recovery from this stage seemed almost impossible. Again, he was fed throughout the night, with a weak mixture of honey and a baby cereal. I thought he missed human contact while in the brooder, and also disliked being in there. Wrapping him in a towel, at 5.15 am, I held him near the fire for an hour or so, rubbing his head all the time. Ill as he was, he liked this and did not vomit. He was then placed in a small cage near the fire with an infra-red lamp for additional heat. If I saw vomiting was about to occur when he was in the cage, I took him out immediately, wrapped him in the towel and rubbed his head. He did not vomit. That morning feeding was difficult for the first time.

By late afternoon he looked much better and had eaten some millet spray. During dinner he insisted on coming out and wolfed down broccoli, something he had never eaten before. Recovery was very apparent, and it seemed that the Framycetin was responsible. This was given twice daily, as well as vitamins and Nystatin on occasions. The anti-fungal preparation was given because treatment with antibiotics makes birds more susceptible to *Candida albicans*.

On the following day the young Grey's eyes were wide open. Previously the slit or half-closed or not fully round eyes were typical of a sick bird. He started to eat corn and millet, apparently ravenously hungry. He vomited a little. Droppings were black, with no urine (white) visible – presumably a result of giving antibiotics. Vomiting had ceased by the following day, he ate constantly, demanded to be fed often and soon regained the lost weight.

It is very distressing to see any bird vomiting continually and close to death; but in a young, affectionate Grey which should have many years ahead of it as a cherished pet it is a heart-rending experience. Bacterial infections are not uncommon in young parrots; bacteria are always present and if the bird is stressed in any way they gain the upper hand.

Several factors should be borne in mind if similar cases occur. First, remember that dehydration is likely, and give very large quantities of liquid at frequent intervals. Do not fail to consult a vet because, as in the case described, an antibiotic, perhaps one of the lesser-known ones, provides the best chance of saving the bird. Also, never give up. No bird could have been closer to death yet survived than this young Grey.

After struggling for life for the first three days, and at 15 weeks, the young Grey became as strong and alert and as well developed as any I had reared. Early setbacks can be overcome if the usual routine is adjusted to suit the individual chick. In this case it meant adapting the diet from the day of hatching until the third day when the usual diet was offered. The normal procedure for rearing Greys was altered because of the following.

1) The chick's yolk sac was not completely absorbed. Raw egg yolk was therefore a major component of the food for the first three days. This richer food was not digested as quickly as the very diluted food normally fed, therefore it was found that feeding hourly, as would normally be the case, was too frequent.

2) As often occurs in chicks which are very weak on hatching, there is no feeding response, that is, the chick does not grasp the spoon. Feeding is therefore difficult and prolonged and achieved only with patience. The spoon is held beneath the tip of the upper mandible and the chick laps a minute amount of food but tires very quickly.

3) When the initial growth is very slow and development retarded, it is necessary to provide a 3 am feed for a longer period, in this case until the age of 18 days. Normally the 3 am feed is dispensed with after three or four days.

Experience with a certain species might lead one to care for a chick according to the usual diary of development instead of treating each one as an individual. Losses will be minimised if the latter approach is adopted.

Some chicks are extremely precious because of their rarity in captivity and their declining and endangered status in the wild. Such was the case of the Yellow-shouldered Amazon (*Amazona barbadensis*) hatched by my pair in 1982. Before that year, this species had never been bred in captivity; and then Ramon Noegel in Florida was also successful.

My pair had never previously hatched a chick, and when their first chick hatched on July 15, as so often happens with Amazons, they were confused and excited and they bit it. It was bruised on the head and bitten on the wing tips and toenails. As soon as it was observed, later that day, it was removed to an incubator until a brooder reached the required temperature of 35° C (95° F). It was sparsely covered with longish white down on the upper parts only, from the nape to the lower back.

The day after hatching it weighed 10 g and for the first five days of its life gained only 1 g daily. The food was a thin mixture of Heinz first weaning food, Bone and Beef Broth with Vegetables (then in packets) and Heinz tinned strained fruit dessert, plus a little bone flour. After five days ground wheat germ cereal was added, plus ground CéDé, a proprietary rearing food, three days later. A couple of days after the CéDé was added the most significant weight gains occurred – 5 g in one day, whereas previously the largest gain had been of 2 g.

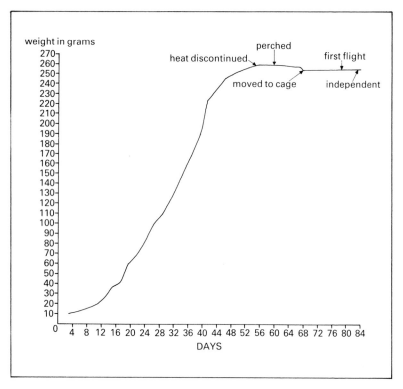

*Fig. 11  Development of Yellow-shouldered Amazon (*Amazona barbadensis*).*

I had deliberately fed a rather poor diet initially as chicks reared from day one are more liable to succumb to an over-rich diet during that period than to an inadequate one. They can, in fact, be kept alive on foods which are nutritionally poor, and it does them no harm for the first few days during which they are most sensitive to over-generous feeding.

The Yellow-shouldered Amazon was not very strong when found but soon gained strength and became easier to feed. At first its voice was a mere squeak and seldom used. After a few days it became stronger vocally, uttering a single staccato note which was repeated six or eight times in rapid succession. Unlike some chicks, which will cry for food even when their crops are bulging, it slept soundly between feeds. By three weeks of age the head bobbing movements made during feeding were very vigorous. Its eyes were late to open: they started to slit at 19 days and were not fully open until 28 days. Such lateness is no cause for concern if the chick is healthy. The wing feathers were the first to emerge, by about the 26th day. By five weeks the raised pads on the sides of the upper mandible were dark and the feathers on the flanks were erupting.

The chick was moved to another brooder where the temperature was lower, approximately 27°C (83°F). It was removed from a box containing kitchen towel and placed on a deep bed of wood shavings. It then feathered up quickly and its feathering was complete by 46 days, except for the short tail. The heat in the brooder had been gradually reduced to about 21°C (70°F) and was discontinued when the young Amazon was 54 days old (early September) when he was moved to a weaning cage. Four days later he started to perch. At 69 days he was moved to a small parrot cage and immediately climbed to the top perch.

He flew for the first time at 77 days, circling the room strongly. He mastered the technique of flying more quickly and with greater accuracy than any parrot I had reared. Some are very clumsy for a while, but within a few days he had acquired the unusual skills of hovering and low diving.

There are very few Yellow-shouldered Amazons in captivity and the proportion of males to females is unfortunately at least 5:1. The rearing of this bird was therefore very important to me: I hoped it would be a female to pair to one of my unmated males. Alas, surgical sexing at two years old established it was a male; but during the rearing period I was not to know this and, of course, watched over it with great concern. At about five weeks old I discovered in his mouth a small yellow area with raised spots on it. My veterinary surgeon took a swab from inside the mouth but laboratory tests revealed nothing but the presence of *E. coli* – a normal finding. He prescribed Clamoxyl sweet-tasting drops, one of which I applied locally and another to the food daily. After a few days of this treatment the infected area diminished. I discontinued the drops and a recurrence was apparent. In all Clamoxyl was given for four weeks without any harmful effects (Low, 1983a).

This young Amazon was weaned by 11½ weeks. The transition to soaked seed and fruit (pomegranate was preferred) was made without any difficulty. Very careful attention had been paid to his diet at all stages and regular examinations made of the inside of the mouth. Nothing must be left to chance; all chicks are valuable but the value of endangered species is incalculable in terms of future breeding potential.

# 9

# UNWEANED YOUNG – A CAUTIONARY STORY

In the USA it is not uncommon for breeders or pet stores to offer unweaned young for sale. Ostensibly the reason is to allow the purchaser to build up a good relationship with the parrot by completing the task of hand-feeding. In reality it is because the seller does not want the task of weaning. At this stage chicks require more attention than at any other, except when newly-hatched, and some become difficult to feed and harder to handle. They may go through a stage of nipping and need to be corrected.

A hand-reared bird bought soon after it has been weaned by the breeder will be as responsive and affectionate to its new owner as one for which weaning has yet to be accomplished.

There are two reasons why the sale of unweaned young should be discouraged.

Firstly, chicks are at their most vulnerable to changes in their environment as they approach and experience the weaning period. To change their surroundings and the faces with which they are familiar must be traumatic and could result in shock and even death. Some birds react adversely to being moved from brooder to weaning cage – so it is not difficult to imagine their reluctance to feed when removed from their siblings and everything with which they have been familiar.

Secondly, someone who has not previously hand-reared parrots is not competent to take on the often difficult task of weaning a parrot. The seller may try to persuade him or her that it is a routine task – but nothing could be further from the truth. In inexperienced hands a chick can be literally starved to death or killed by overfeeding. The unnecessary suffering to bird and owner is almost beyond belief.

I will describe one such case, in the hope that it will prevent similar tragic losses. A lady bought a seven-week-old Amazon parrot from a pet store, with instructions on its feeding and care. After an unspecified period the young Amazon was checked by a veterinarian and found to have a 'bacterial infection'. It was given injections and the infection was believed to have been cleared up. This was eight weeks after purchase when the excellent weight of 425 g was recorded.

The owner noted: 'As the weeks went on, she got bigger, grew her feathers, and became a major part of my life. She was the centre of my attention. We'd play for hours; we'd "snuggle" and take naps together. I would put a satin sheet on the couch, so in the afternoon sometimes she could take a nap in style! She'd climb two flights of stairs, just so that she could be with me. I loved her so very much. . .'.

However, there was a serious problem: by the time she was 17 weeks old she would not eat on her own. The pet store had suggested putting seed in a dish in her cage and soaked monkey chow in another dish, and hand-feeding her pieces of food. This did not succeed. When she was 17 weeks old the owner attempted to consult the vet who had treated her, but he was not available. Another vet told her that the bird was 'spoiled rotten' and that the number of feeds should be reduced from two to one per day as she was being overfed. This was suggested over the telephone; the parrot was not examined.

This was poor advice. No bird receiving only two feeds per day is overfed. A healthy bird would suffer enough hunger between these feeds to encourage it to start feeding itself. No matter how many feeds are offered to a young parrot at weaning age, it will normally attempt to pick up and swallow food left in its cage. The fact that it failed to do so suggests that something was wrong and that the vet should have examined the bird and obtained a sample of its faeces.

The advice to feed only once per day, as well as to leave pellets in its cage, was followed. (Pellets are not an attractive food. Young birds require soft, tasty items.) After one week the owner was instructed to feed once a day but only half-fill the Amazon's crop; she was told that by then she would be weaned. The owner protested that the bird would die of starvation and was advised that this would not occur.

On April 22 the vet was again consulted because the young Amazon refused to sample the pellets. Her weight had dropped drastically to 334 g. This was described as 'a little underweight' by the vet. By then she was sleeping much of the time, drinking excessively and had regurgitated food on two occasions. The owner was very concerned, realising that the bird was very ill and asked for X-rays and blood tests, but the vet assured her 'there was nothing wrong'. He insisted she was spoiled and suggested a new formula, consisting of three parts pellets, one part monkey chow, one part honey, plus water.

By April 23 her droppings had become like 'black tar', but again the vet stated that this was not an indication of ill health, when nothing could have been further from the truth. By April 25 the original veterinary consultant had returned and immediately took the Amazon into the animal hospital. She weighed 308 g. A bacterial infection was discovered and X-rays and blood tests made, as well as gram stains. She was tube-fed five times daily. She continued to regurgitate food and to lose weight and died on May 3, weighing 284 g. Cause of death was established as starvation and kidney failure. Her right kidney was found to be enlarged to twice the normal size, and her left kidney was three times larger than usual due to the bacterial infection.

I would appeal to breeders not to sell unweaned young to pet shops in any circumstances. The purchaser will not know who to turn to if problems arise. Only the breeder is competent to advise on its care, and pet shops are not likely to encourage contact between buyer and breeder. Those who sell unweaned young may be condemning them to death through sheer ignorance on the part of the purchaser.

*Twenty Queen of Bavaria's (Golden) Conures* (Aratinga guarouba),
*hand-reared from the egg by Jim and Pearl Hayward in 1983.*

*Swainson's Lorikeet*
(Trichoglossus haematodus
moluccanus), *day 1.*

*Swainson's Lorikeet, day 7.*

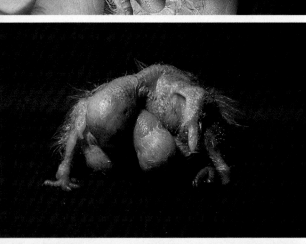

*Swainson's Lorikeet, day 10.*

*Swainson's Lorikeet, day 16.*

*Swainson's Lorikeet, day 19.*

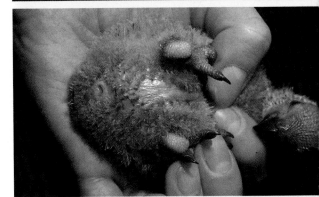

*Swainson's Lorikeet, day 20.*

*Swainson's Lorikeet, day 29.*

*Swainson's Lorikeet, day 57.*

*Umbrella Cockatoo* (Cacatua alba) *aged 19 days, weighing 140 g and taking 8 g at each feed.*

*Umbrella Cockatoo aged 37 days, weighing 318 g and taking 24 g at each feed.*

*Umbrella Cockatoo aged 57 days, weighing 416 g and taking about 40 g at each feed.*

*Nest of four Red-browed Amazons (Amazona rhodocorytha) hand-reared by Mrs Pat Mann in 1984. The parents are the most prolific captive pair of this endangered species.*

*Feeding an Iris Lorikeet* (Trichoglossus iris), *aged 15 days.*

*For very young chicks a plastic spoon (sides bent inwards) is to be preferred to the silver one seen here, because the surface is softer.*

*These two female Eclectus* (Eclectus roratus vosmaeri) *had to be removed from the nest when the parents stopped feeding them during a sudden bitterly cold spell in December.*

*Hand-reared Grey Parrots (Psittacus erithacus), such as this one aged 8 weeks, grow up to be much tamer and more demanding pets than those which are parent-reared.*

*Blue-streaked (Eos reticulata) and Black-capped (Lorius lory lory) Lories which were hand-reared together. For weeks, the growth of the bird on the left was retarded but it had developed into a fine bird by the time it was weaned.*

*Male Eclectus Parrot* (Eclectus roratus vosmaeri), *aged about 5 weeks. This is the only large parrot which can be sexed as soon as the feathers appear.*

*The first Yellow-shouldered Amazon* (Amazona barbadensis) *reared in the UK (see Chapter 8) and a Queen of Bavaria's Conure* (Aratinga guarouba) *( see Chapter 6 ).*

# 10

# CARE AND FUTURE OF HAND-REARED PARROTS

The proud and delighted owner of a hand-reared parrot, obtained as a pet, will need some guidance regarding its care and handling. This differs from that of young parrots which are wild-caught, or even those which are aviary-bred and reared by their parents. Patience and caution are usually necessary in these cases, because the young birds are nervous, and forcing one's attention on them can do more harm than good. Initially, the emphasis must be on obtaining the bird's confidence. Many imported birds are afraid of hands and attempts to make them step on to the hand are detrimental to their training.

## PERIODS OF LIBERTY

In contrast, a hand-reared parrot is afraid of nothing and no-one, and its natural exuberance and curiosity can lead it into trouble. Young parrots which are hand-reared and therefore full-flighted (in contrast to imported birds, many of which have had their flight feathers cut) are extremely strong flyers. Soon after they learn to fly, during the weaning period, they are capable of circling the room at great speed. Unfortunately, their skill in landing is less advanced and, at first, they may need to be caught in flight to prevent possible injury. Do not be misled into believing that a tame young parrot will not fly far – and do not give it an opportunity to find out!

I am opposed to cutting the flight feathers of pet parrots to prevent their escape. The power of flight is a great source of enjoyment and a beneficial form of exercise for which there is no substitute. Tame birds will be unhappy if deprived of this.

However, the danger of escape is ever-present. A moment's carelessness can result in the loss (and, in all probability, the death) of a greatly-cherished pet, followed by months of remorse. The owner of a tame bird which is allowed its liberty in the room must get into the habit of closing doors and windows at all times. If this is inconvenient in the summer, a wire-mesh-covered frame can be fitted over windows.

The danger of escape is especially great with hand-reared birds which enjoy being carried around on their owner's shoulder. This can become such a habit that he or she walks outside, forgetting the parrot is there. The bird becomes alarmed by unfamiliar sights or sounds and takes off in panic. This, regrettably, was the fate of one of my hand-reared Greys which had been with her new owner for a couple of years. She was never seen again. The heartbreak that such an experience causes and the sense of loss to the owner can never be forgotten.

With such tame birds one cannot afford a moment's inattention when they are loose in the room. They are inquisitive and this trait can lead to accidents. Before letting a tame parrot out, take a good look round and view all items as a possible source of danger. Cover fish tanks, remove pot plants that may be poisonous, and never let a bird loose in the kitchen when cooking is in progress. Ensure that non-stick coated pans do not overheat as the fumes are lethal to birds and have been responsible for the deaths of many pets. These points may seem obvious – but failure to apply common sense, or becoming blasé because a parrot is not usually adventurous, have resulted in the death or injury of countless birds.

## OTHER PETS

Hand-reared parrots have no fear of animals and will often exert their dominance over cats and dogs. While house pets generally accept this, visiting dogs may be less tolerant.

## LOVE AND ATTENTION

Hand-reared parrots will take over the household if their owner lets them. Initially, they may be spoiled, being allowed out of the cage at every demand. (Greys which I have hand-reared have all developed the habit, just after weaning, of scratching on the floor with impatience.) This is unwise; from the outset they should have set periods of liberty in the room, perhaps an hour every morning and longer in the evening, or whatever suits the owner.

They do need a great deal of attention, far more than imported young parrots which are less demanding. Some species, such as Moluccan Cockatoos and Hyacinthine Macaws, can be quite as demanding as a child; and no-one should take one on unless they have a great deal of time to spend with the bird. If it does not receive the required attention it may start to nip or develop other undesirable habits.

A bird whose owner can devote a great deal of time to just being with it will develop a wonderful bond with one or more members of the family. Another advantage of hand-reared parrots is that they can be handled by anyone, even complete strangers. This should be encouraged, rather than allowing the bird to become the pet of one individual. Many birds, however, develop a marked preference for one person, even to the exclusion of all others, so that they refuse other overtures of friendship as they mature. There is nothing that one can do about this. They may even behave aggressively towards those who are not in favour.

For the breeder who hand-rears Greys the problem is not in selling the young but in finding truly suitable homes where the birds will be fully appreciated. It is very satisfying to know how great a source of enjoyment is a young parrot which one has reared from the day it hatched and which one parts with somewhat reluctantly. A young man who purchased just such a Grey Parrot from me wrote to say: 'I knew that a hand-reared bird was something special but really did not understand how special. I am glad I took my impatience in hand and waited for one to turn up.'

However, new owners are disappointed if their birds show traits they had not expected, such as biting. Even though given all the love and attention necessary, some parrots develop the habit of biting. Some can be cured by a sharp 'No!' and a tap on the beak, and even returning it to its cage. Others can never grow out of this habit and the owner may tolerate it until it is mature enough to breed, when a mate can be obtained. Perhaps then they will be able to breed for themselves the ideal pet which never bites.

## DIET

Those who buy hand-reared parrots should, of course, obtain a young bird which has been weaned onto seed. However, the fact that it eats seed does not mean that this has to form the main part of its diet. One of the advantages of hand-reared youngsters, unlike an imported one, is that they are very ready to sample all manner of foods. While they are young their experience of foods can be expanded greatly; adult birds are much less easily persuaded to try new items. Therefore, a very wide range of fruits, vegetables and human foods can be offered. The latter can include breakfast cereals with milk, cheese, lean meat, toast, biscuits, cooked vegetables and yoghurt. Also offer a good variety of seeds and nuts, sprouted mung beans and sprouted sunflower seed.

The life-span of a parrot is greatly influenced by the diet, which should be varied and nutritious and not greatly reliant on seed. If fed correctly, and well cared for, your hand-reared parrot will be a friend for life.

## MIMICRY

In hand-reared birds the ability to mimic is often apparent at a very early age. The human voice is the first sound of any significance to those hand-fed from a few days old, thus there are plenty of instances of chicks talking before they are weaned. In addition, species not renowned for their ability to mimic learn to do so early on. One man who hand-reared a Golden-mantled Rosella (*Platycercus eximius*) from four days old reported to me that 'Goldie', as it was called, was repeating its name and saying 'Come on' very distinctly, soon after weaning. In another case, a Thick-billed Parrot (*Rhynchopsitta pachyrhyncha*), could repeat 'Hello' at only 57 days, at about which age it would have left the nest if parent-reared, and a Yellow-billed Amazon repeated the same word at 74 days.

## BREEDING

Many hand-reared youngsters will not be kept as pets but be used for breeding. This is vitally important in the case of rare and endangered species, and also important for the more common ones to ensure the future of aviculture. Importations of wild-caught birds will not continue indefinitely; the export of fauna has been prohibited or greatly reduced by many tropical countries. The proportion of hand-reared to parent-reared young increases every year. In the USA probably more young of the larger parrots are reared by hand than by their parents. If all these youngsters were kept as pets and denied the opportunity to breed, ultimately there would not be enough breeding pairs to safeguard the future of parrot breeding.

Aviculturists should therefore seek the co-operation of other breeders so that, instead of selling most of their hand-reared young as pets, they make up unrelated pairs to sell as potential breeding stock. Alternatively, they should maintain more than one breeding pair of each species so that they themselves are in a position to sell unrelated pairs. Almost invariably there are surplus males, and these can be sold as pets.

Young which are to be used for breeding should be kept with members of their own species, or their own genus if this is not possible, soon after they are weaned. On no account should they be returned to the aviary occupied by their parents. Almost certainly they would be attacked as intruders. Ideally, single birds would be placed with other young birds or, failing that, young adults or unmated adults. Before doing this, however, they must be adjusted to life in an aviary. Initially this means one not inhabited by other birds so that they can acquire confidence in strange surroundings without being harassed by older birds, especially those who consider the aviary their own territory. It is for this reason that

*This male Eclectus Parrot (*Eclectus roratus vosmaeri*), reared by the author, is just weaned, but he will not be going anywhere. He will be retained for breeding purposes. All aviculturists should keep back a proportion of their young for this reason.*

an older bird should be introduced into the aviary of the young one, and not vice versa. Compatibility may be a problem when adult birds are introduced, but this is unlikely when two young birds, a potential breeding pair, are put together.

The myth that hand-reared birds are useless for breeding is gradually being dispelled; in the 1980s it has been disproved on countless occasions, some of them by second and third generations of hand-reared birds. Most hand-reared parrots have little fear of man or other birds; this greatly reduces the likelihood of them suffering from any stress-induced condition. The latter leads to more diseases and nesting failures than most breeders realise.

The only hand-reared birds which are a poor prospect for breeding are those which are kept on their own as pets from the time they are weaned. They become imprinted on humans and some (but not all) prove useless for breeding.

If properly cared for, hand-reared birds equal or excel those raised by their parents in every respect. With the exception of most Australian parrakeets which, when hand-reared and placed in an aviary, usually lose their tameness, the confidence of hand-reared birds means that they provide much more pleasure and satisfaction. After all, who wants to keep birds which fly off when one approaches?

In some quarters, in Britain and Europe, there is still prejudice against hand-reared birds. Some avicultural societies will not award first breeding medals for successes which result from hand-rearing. With respect, they have missed the point. It matters not whether a bird is hand-reared or parent-reared, only that it is a fine, healthy specimen which is capable of reproducing in captivity. The breeder who hand-rears birds which will be used for this purpose deserves recognition: he or she is helping to ensure the future of aviculture. The breeder who sells parent-reared young of the rarer species as pets is doing no such thing. It should be obvious which one deserves a medal.

Let me make it clear that I am not totally against hand-rearing young to be sold as pets. With common species, such as Grey Parrots, the sale of such birds could eventually result in fewer young being taken from the wild, although I suspect that import and/or export controls will have this effect before sufficient are bred in captivity.

What I could never condone is the sale of young of such species as Queen of Bavaria's (Golden) Conures and Hyacinthine Macaws as pets. Breeding successes are not plentiful enough to ensure the survival of rare species in captivity unless the great majority of the young are retained for breeding purposes.

# 11

# ARTIFICIAL INCUBATION

There comes the day when every breeder wishes that he or she possessed an incubator. If there is no foster parent available for an abandoned fertile egg it means that the chick is doomed to die – unless, of course, an incubator is available. No serious breeder can afford to be without an incubator. They are fairly expensive pieces of equipment, but their cost will almost certainly be recouped within a short time if the breeder is prepared to hand-rear chicks from the egg or can find someone to do it for him or her.

It is important to realise that, unless today's breeders establish captive-bred strains of foreign birds, many species will be unknown to tomorrow's aviculturists. The 1980s could be looked back upon as the decade of lost opportunity unless we use every means at our disposal to rear more and more young. Thus every serious breeder intent on furthering aviculture must be in possession of an incubator.

## TYPES OF INCUBATOR

First of all any ideas of constructing your own should be dismissed – except by a skilled electrician. Still-air incubators are obsolete pieces of equipment. Today there is a choice of small forced-air incubators on the market which will suit the breeder who is unlikely to have more than half a dozen eggs inside it at any one time; although, of course, the capacity of the smallest model is 50 or so eggs.

The incubator should not be kept in a room which is very susceptible to fluctuations of temperature, such as a kitchen. An unheated, unused room is ideal. Do not place the incubator near a window where the temperature could be influenced by the rays of the sun and cause the eggs to become overheated.

Choose an incubator with the heat source in the centre so that heat is evenly distributed. If this is not the case, place a thermometer as near

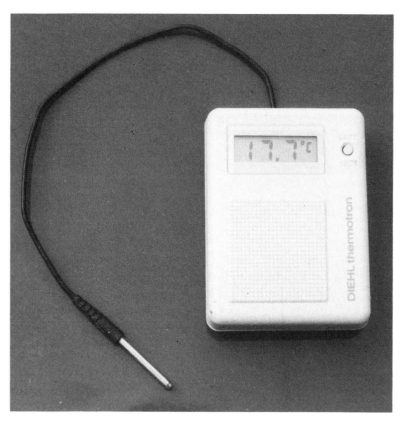

*For accuracy and for an instant read-out, the digital thermometer is unsurpassed in incubator or brooder.*

to the eggs as possible. To safeguard against a faulty model when an ordinary mercury thermometer is used, place two thermometers inside. If necessary, drill a hole in the top or side of the incubator, so that the bulb or probe is close to the eggs. Better still, go to the expense of obtaining an electronic thermometer, an invaluable piece of equipment with a digital read-out to one decimal place. Ensure that the battery is replaced when necessary (frequently using the battery test button). Electronic thermometers have a probe which can be placed right next to the egg, the thermometer itself being outside the incubator.

It is vitally important that one has an accurate reading of the temperature within the incubator. Some models have the thermometer mounted behind a glass window; it may register a different temperature to that surrounding the eggs. The thermometer and humidity gauge on some incubators leave a lot to be desired because they are difficult to read, or cheap thermometers are used with increments of more than 1° F which do not give the necessary accuracy.

Parrot eggs should be incubated at between 36.9° C and 37.5° C (98.5° F and 99.5° F) in forced-air incubators. A still-air incubator is not recommended because the temperature tends to fluctuate unacceptably; if used the temperature would need to be 2 or 3° F higher.

Humidity is equally as important as temperature; excessive humidity causes the death of chicks before and after hatching. It is responsible for chicks pipping the shell prematurely, or pipping but failing to hatch. It can cause an oedema (swollen tissue containing fluid) on the chick's neck which proves such a hindrance that the chick is unable to reach the shell with its egg tooth. Unless assisted to hatch, it will die (Fentzloff, 1984). If a chick is heard calling strongly at first, but its voice gradually becomes weaker, assisted hatching is essential if it is to be saved.

In the unlikely event of humidity within the incubator or hatcher being too low, the shell could become brittle, so that when the chick starts to hatch the initial hole it makes is too large. The inside of the egg dries out, including the shell membrane, to which the chick adheres. It is thus unable to rotate to hatch, and will die unless assisted. This could also occur if the shell is too thin.

If in doubt it is better to err on the side of too low humidity, with little or no water in the incubator. The humidity in most households is in the region of 65 per cent, and greater humidity than this is not generally required until a chick pips the shell, i.e. it makes the first little dent which indicates that (with luck) hatching is imminent. It is probable that most parrot eggs require in the region of 50 per cent relative humidity (84 degrees dry bulb reading) until pipping, when the humidity should be increased very greatly. If there is only one egg in the incubator or the other eggs have also pipped, the eggs can remain in the incubator, but otherwise the pipping eggs must be removed to a hatcher or brooder to prevent eggs at earlier stages of incubation absorbing too much moisture if the humidity is increased.

In order to read humidity quickly and easily I use a combined hygrometer and thermometer (made by Casella, London) which measures only 7 cm (3½ in) in diameter, placed on the incubator grid. A digital thermometer (Diehl Thermotron) is used to double-check the temperature. This is not, of course, necessary, but I can be confident that the temperature and humidity readings are totally accurate.

To avoid opening the incubator, check with a torch to see if the egg has pipped. Once an egg has pipped, it should no longer be turned. Most incubators have automatic turning devices; some have manual devices but, whichever is the case, it means that eggs can be turned without opening the incubator and allowing air to escape, thus lowering the temperature. Incubators such as Marsh Farms (Marsh Mfg Inc, 7171 Paterson Drive, Garden Grove, Ca 92641, USA) Turn-X and Roll-X (two very popular models) have turning grids which are available in different sizes. The small size is recommended for the parrot keeper who will probably be handling eggs of various sizes, as it can turn eggs smaller or larger than the optimum size. Manual turning can be carried out, if desired, by unplugging the turning device.

Commercially-produced incubators generally have clear domes so that one can observe the eggs without opening the incubator. After an egg has been incubated for a few days, a darker appearance will be apparent if it is fertile. There is no need to remove the egg from the incubator to ascertain this; there is a possibility that it has become addled, resulting in a darker but mottled appearance, but this is less likely in artificially-incubated eggs than in those left with the female, in which addling is often due to the eggs cooling after being left too long. It is quite easy to check progress within the egg using a pen torch (or, by those who reside in the USA, using a flexible transilluminator – a high intensity, pre-focused bulb on a 25 cm, 10 in, shaft, from Medical Diagnostic Services, Brandon, Florida).

Some experienced breeders weigh eggs during incubation to ascertain that the correct weight loss is occurring and adjust the humidity accordingly. This is based on the fact that an egg normally loses 16 per cent of its weight during incubation. The rate of loss can be controlled by raising or lowering the humidity. However, there is little point in doing

*Fig. 12   Humidity during incubation.*

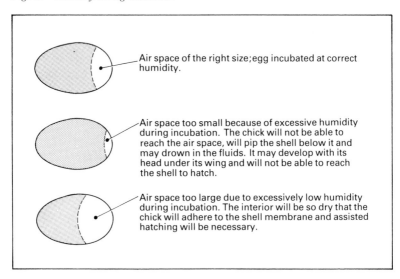

Air space of the right size; egg incubated at correct humidity.

Air space too small because of excessive humidity during incubation. The chick will not be able to reach the air space, will pip the shell below it and may drown in the fluids. It may develop with its head under its wing and will not be able to reach the shell to hatch.

Air space too large due to excessively low humidity during incubation. The interior will be so dry that the chick will adhere to the shell membrane and assisted hatching will be necessary.

this unless one has several incubators, or unless there is only one egg in the incubator or all the eggs therein have the same humidity requirements.

Hopefully, the foregoing has not given the impression that the artificial incubation of eggs is difficult or requires technical expertise. It is mainly a question of ensuring that the temperature is correct and remains constant. The same also applies to humidity.

## HYGIENE

Between each hatch the incubator must be sterilised or fumigated. The importance of choosing a model which is easy to clean will then be discovered. Those made of wood or polystyrene should be avoided because they are difficult to clean and, unless fumigated, could harbour harmful bacteria. Fumigation is recommended for all incubators, using formalin (37 per cent formaldehyde solution), which can be ordered from chemists, and potassium permanganate crystals. Place a teaspoonful of formaldehyde and a pinch of the crystals in a dish inside the incubator and replace the lid very quickly. The gas which it gives off is powerful! Leave for 24 hours.

Cleanliness of the incubator and the egg is very important; unhygienic conditions can lead to chicks dying as the result of a yolk sac infection.

*A seemingly healthy newly-hatched Eclectus Parrot (*Eclectus roratus vosmaeri*). It was dead the next day, a victim of bacterial invasion due to the incubator not being fumigated between hatches.*

107

Death occurs at an early age, usually before five days. Chicks may look healthy on hatching and the breeder may be mystified regarding the cause of death unless a post-mortem examination is carried out.

Losses occur because bacteria gain access to the yolk sac which is absorbed into the chick's body shortly before hatching. The bacteria multiply within the yolk, then invade the bloodstream causing a generalised bacterial toxaemia and death. The bacteria invasion can occur before the chick hatches, causing full-term dead-in-shell. Bacterial contamination of the eggshell can occur while the egg is in the nest or in the incubator, but eggs are most susceptible during a period of cooling. Contraction of contents then takes place and bacteria present on the shell surface can be drawn through the pores of the shell. Thus eggs which have been deserted, then placed in an incubator, are more likely to be subject to hatching failure and the reason will not be clear.

Bacterial invasion can also occur through the unhealed navel of a chick, especially if the humidity has been too great during the incubation period. Imperfect healing of the navel and inflammation will be evident. In this case the navel should be treated with an antibacterial powder obtainable from a veterinarian. Other abdominal organs may be affected and swelling of the abdomen is noticeable.


## ASSISTED HATCHING

Sometimes it is necessary to assist a chick to hatch – but not necessarily due to any weakness on the part of the chick which usually turns out to be a perfect strong specimen. The problem may be faulty incubation technique, i.e. excessive humidity in the incubator which, as already mentioned, causes the chick to pip but not hatch, or the chick may be unable to escape from the shell because the membrane between the chick and the shell dries on to the chick, preventing it from rotating within the shell.

Knowledge of the date on which an egg was laid is invaluable in deciding whether or not to help a chick out of the shell. Alas, this information is seldom available. If the decision is made to remove eggs to an incubator, they should be numbered as laid. If this is not possible, examination with a pen torch should provide a good idea as to the stage that their development has reached; but, except in the case of a specialist in incubation, this examination will not provide the answer to the date on which hatching is due.

The decision may be made to assist a chick if, after about 36–48 hours after the first pip mark appears, there is no further progress. A small hole should be made in the air space at the large end of the egg; one can then see if the chick has penetrated the air space and is therefore breathing air.

If it has, there may be no great urgency as chicks can exist for a couple of days or more. The only deaths I have experienced after removing chicks from the egg were two which were long overdue. In one amazing case it was 31 days after the egg had been laid and the normal incubation period was 24 days for this species, a Meyer's Lorikeet. In the other instance, involving a Grey Parrot, the excessive dryness within the egg, which meant the shell could be peeled off in seconds, and the large amount of faeces, also indicated the chick was long overdue. It was very weak and died soon after.

The main danger in assisted hatching is that the chick is removed too soon. This will almost certainly result in its death because the shell membrane is punctured, damaging blood vessels and causing the chick to bleed. If blood is visible after some of the shell has been removed the chick is not ready to hatch and it should be replaced in a brooder with high humidity for at least 24 hours. Even if as much as half of the shell has been peeled off the chick may survive; but it will not do so if one progresses as the blood loss will be too great.

The procedure for removing a chick from the egg is not as complicated as might be thought. All that is required is a needle, warm water, a small hair paintbrush – and common sense. First, chip away a small amount of shell to expose the beak. After the removal of a little more shell do not proceed if blood vessels are visible.

Where the chick's body is against the membrane of the egg, moisten the membrane using the hair brush and warm water, sliding the brush between membrane and chick. Do not let the chick cool; return to the brooder and proceed further after about 15 minutes. Continue in this way until all the shell has been removed, provided that the chick appears to be ready to hatch.

Mention was made above of a Meyer's Lorikeet released from the egg 31 days after it was laid. The female had been breeding for several years and always started incubation when the first egg was laid. It was extremely unlikely that the start of incubation had been delayed. The pair were breeding in a brick building and excessive humidity, causing premature pipping, was impossible.

The nest was checked daily during the week in which the egg should have hatched. It was not until 31 days, however, that I was able to inspect the egg properly and saw a small pip mark. I assumed that the chick had tried to hatch and had died. I took the egg indoors and made a small hole with a pin near the mark. I saw a vein – then movement! I carefully removed small pieces of shell by the beak. I could see the beak opening and closing; the chick was gulping air.

I could see blood between the shell and the membrane which made me fearful that the chick was not ready to hatch – but this was surely impossible. It was obviously very weak and did not cheep.

My husband assisted me in releasing the chick. With a small hair brush and water he moistened the membrane adhering to the chick while I removed small pieces of shell. After a couple of minutes the egg/chick was cold and was returned to the brooder at 32.2° C (90° F). Ten minutes later it was removed and a little more shell peeled off. This process was continued until after about one hour one wing and one leg were free of the shell. There was little movement from the chick. When half the shell had been removed, about one-and-a-half hours after starting the operation, it was possible to gently prise off the remaining shell intact, without any loss of blood. There was no doubt that the chick was overdue by several days due to the large quantity of faeces and the total lack of air space. I dusted the umbilicus with antibiotic powder and placed the chick in the brooder.

It lay there scarcely breathing, and the chances that it would survive seemed slim. It had to be watched over continually and the body temperature continually tested by touch for the first hour or so to ensure that it did not become overheated. However, the problem at first was that it seemed cold.

About one hour later I dripped glucose dissolved in hot water on to the side of its beak; the chick was laying on its side and much too weak to raise its head. The reaction was immediate. Its tiny throat could be seen working. It could suck in the water in minute quantities. It was then 5 pm. Every 30 to 60 minutes I gave three or four drops of glucose solution. By 9 pm it was on its feet!

It was still too weak for spoon-feeding to be attempted. Also, it quickly lost heat when removed from the brooder. Throughout the night glucose was given every two hours. By early morning it was strong enough to feed from a spoon. Greatly diluted food (tinned Heinz Pure Fruit and Bone and Beef Broth) was given. The chick was easily exhausted and could take only very small quantities of food. For the first 12 hours or so there was much air in its crop, but this soon dispersed. That day it needed intensive care, and I took a day's holiday from my job in order to feed it every 45 to 60 minutes. It was encouraging to see it gradually gaining strength. Its weight was 4 g, the normal hatching weight for this species.

By the next day its weight had increased to 4.5 g. It had taken on a healthy and fluffy appearance, whereas the previous day the down on the head was still plastered together and lay flat. It seemed to progress well until the age of five days when it died. This was a bitter disappointment after working so hard for its survival. However, all those who hand-rear chicks on a regular basis have to accept that there will be losses, despite the most intensive care. I can only assume that its death was due to the fact that its brain had been starved of oxygen during the time it was in the egg, after it had used the oxygen in the air space. If it had been released 24 hours previously the outcome might have been success.

After releasing a chick from the shell, the first step is to puff some veterinary antibacterial dressing powder on the navel. If the yolk sac has not been fully absorbed and is still outside the body, there may be problems, but there is nothing you can do except leave it alone. After a few days, if the chick survives, it will dry up and fall off.

## FEEDING

A question often asked is: how soon after hatching should a chick be fed? If hatching has been prolonged or difficult it can do no harm to feed glucose dissolved in hot water as soon as the chick is strong enough to take it. If the chick is too weak to hold up its head minute amounts can be dripped into the side of the beak using an eye dropper or the dropper from a bottle of liquid vitamins. Liquid is more important than food; the chick must have this to prevent dehydration.

Strong chicks can be fed with a very diluted solution of the food to be used as soon after hatching as is convenient, i.e. one to three hours. I have seen advice that chicks need not be fed until 48 hours after hatching. While it is true that their yolk sac could sustain them for this length of time, there is nothing to be gained from leaving chicks unfed, because the danger of dehydration would be great.

## TEMPERATURE

For the first 24 hours great attention must be paid to the thermometer within the brooder to ensure that the heat source is maintaining an even temperature. Newly-hatched chicks cannot tolerate high temperatures for more than a very few minutes, so you must be ever on guard against overheating. This is one reason why attending to the chick at 3 am on the first night is so important because it may be necessary to adjust the temperature. It is better to err on the side of a temperature which is very slightly too low rather than slightly too high, because a chick takes much longer to die from cooling than from overheating.

## APPEARANCE OF CHICKS

Chicks of various species differ considerably in appearance on hatching. Neotropical parrots have fleshy raised pads on each side of the upper mandible, which remain for several weeks. Most cockatoos, also Grey Parrots, have wide, shovel-like lower mandibles which are quite different to other species, such as lories, in which the beak shape is the same as

*Fig. 13 Different beak shapes. 1. Slender-billed Conure at 4½ weeks. The beak is still short. Note the raised pad on the side of the upper mandible, typical of neotropical species. 2. Queen of Bavaria's (Golden) Conure. The beak is massive. Note the raised pad. 3. Eclectus Parrot at 5 weeks. The beak is less curved than an adult's. 4. Grey Parrot at 4 weeks. The lower mandible no longer appears disproportionately wide. 5. Cockatiel. This, like most Cockatoos, has a distinctive curve to the cutting edge of the upper mandible.*

that of the adult's. The tiny egg tooth on the upper mandible may be apparent for as long as three weeks. In some species it contrasts with the colour of the bill (e.g. white in Grey Parrots, contrasting with the dark brown bill, Low 1982a).

The order in which feathers appear also differs, but those covering the crop are the last of the contour feathers to erupt in many species. The down differs in colour (usually white or grey, pink in Roseate Cockatoos and lovebirds, and yellow in most cockatoos), length or profuseness according to species. The first down wears off after a few days and is replaced by second down, denser in most species (grey in lories and Eclectus, for example, and white in Grey Parrots). Most are well covered in the second down when the feathers start to erupt. Cockatoos are an exception; they are porcupine-like when the contour feathers appear, for, at that stage, there is no down to conceal the spiky appearance.

*The second down varies according to species; in Eclectus Parrots it is dark grey and dense.*

Most true parrots and cockatoos have a very solid appearance, but some Australian parrakeets, for example, do not. Betty Byers (1984) described the normal thin chicks of Princess of Wales Parrakeets (*Polytelis alexandrae*) as looking 'like a featherless flamingo with their thin legs and necks and their thin bodies'.

In all parrot chicks the opening of the eye is a very gradual process; for example, in those which spend about 11 weeks in the nest, the eyes may start to slit at about 12 days, but it is not until about three weeks that they are fully open (Low, 1984). If one looks very carefully, the first slit marks may be seen as early as one week. I have known cases in which the eyes start to open, then close up again, but eventually open normally. This can happen in perfectly healthy chicks.

*In Grey Parrots* (Psittacus erithacus) *the second down is short, dense on the body, and white. This chick is four weeks old.*

Finally, remember that chicks will require very frequent attention for the first few days of their lives. Unless you can find someone to deputise in your absence, your social life will have to be re-arranged to meet their requirements. However, the satisfaction gained in rearing a chick from the egg, in knowing when it is weaned, that its survival has been entirely dependent upon your care and skill, is of a very special kind. Some breeders find the task too demanding and time-consuming – but for the most sensitive and dedicated breeders, the experience is a joyful one to be repeated over and over again, at every opportunity.

# 12

# HAND-REARING SEEDEATERS, SOFTBILLS AND BIRDS OF PREY

Softbills and seed-eating birds (hardbills) are not often hand-reared by aviculturists. When this does occur, it is usually the result of necessity, rather than design. With seedeaters, breeders are more likely to use foster parents (especially Bengalese, also known as Society Finches) than to attempt to hand-rear. It is very rarely that softbills are fostered to other nests, mainly because they are not kept on a large scale and the chances of pairs of related species nesting synchronously are slight. Therefore, despite the far larger numbers of seedeaters kept, it is probably more common for softbills to be hand-reared than seedeaters.

## SEEDEATERS

Many breeders would not attempt to rear seedeating birds, such as finches, because the chicks are so small and look very delicate. However, the principal differences to rearing parrot chicks are that they need feeding very frequently and the nestling stage is very short. Most fledge by three weeks of age, although they need to be fed for a slightly longer period. They are no more delicate than parrot chicks provided that they are cared for correctly. The information already given on general aspects of hand-rearing, such as brooders, temperature requirements and care of chicks, applies equally to softbills and hardbills.

The area where care of these young differs appreciably is feeding, both as regards the implement and the diet. The other point is that the chicks gape to be fed, unlike parrots, and it may be necessary to stimulate them to do so. This is usually easy.

An efficient method for feeding the chicks of Firefinches (*Lagonosticta rubricata*), and Waxbills about 10 cm (4 in) in length, was devised by Mr and Mrs Eastman of Devon, England. The instrument used was a 13 cm (5 in) length of stainless steel tube, approximately 3 mm (⅛ in) in diameter. Into this a number 10 (3.25 mm) knitting needle, cut to 15 cm (6 in) made a sliding fit. A spring from a ballpoint pen was slid over the shank of the knitting needle to come up against the needle head, before being inserted into the stainless steel tube to act as a return for the needle, which then acts as a plunger. The end of the tube was tapered to 45° so that, when placed against the side of the chick's beak, the mandibles could be carefully prised apart for hand-feeding.

The tube was filled from a large syringe. After the end of the tapered tube was in the chick's mouth it was turned through 90° in order to line up with the bird's gullet and the plunger was gently pushed to force the food into the throat (Eastman, 1982).

One of the few British breeders who regularly hand-rears seedeaters is Jim Madden of Northampton. His method results in almost 100 per cent success if the chicks are removed after the seventh day. Australian finches and parrot finches are reared using a 1 ml plastic syringe. The point is sharpened with a pencil sharpener and the aperture drilled out to prevent clogging. A 10 ml or 15 ml syringe is used to charge the smaller one. No air must be trapped in the syringe, and a small amount of food is left in the tube each time it is used to prevent the intake of air. The tube must contain a solid mass of food – and no air. The plunger is worked in the palm of the hand and gripped between the index and middle finger. It is depressed very slowly. The syringe is rested on the side of the mouth, putting a slight pressure on the chick's gape. The food is first heated by placing the container in hot water (Emslie, 1985).

The implements recommended by Frank Meaden, author of the definitive *A Manual of European Bird Keeping*, are an icing syringe, adapting the nozzle by enlarging the small round hole, or, for the inexperienced feeder, a spatula. The latter takes more time but is safer; the food should be placed as far down the throat as possible when the chick is gaping. A syringe can choke a chick in inexperienced hands. If used, the nozzle must be pointed well down the throat on the bird's right-hand side towards the crop.

Food for seedeater chicks usually consists of a proprietary rearing food and seed. For example, the Firefinches referred to earlier in the chapter were on Haith's egg biscuit food (a Canary rearing food), Sluis Universal (proprietary softbill food), panicum millet and half a teaspoonful of honey diluted in water. The Sluis and the panicum millet were prepared in a liquidiser, with water added to give a runny consistency.

The food used to rear Australian finches by Jim Madden consisted of the following: half a pint of sausage rusk, a heaped teaspoonful of Phillips Yeast Mixture (brewer's yeast could be used instead) mixed with half a pint of boiled water and a dessertspoonful of honey to a crumbly consistency; after the mixture had cooled, three heaped teaspoonfuls each of wheat germ cereal and crumbled digestive biscuit were added, and a dessertspoonful of equal parts of blue maw and niger seed. For very young chicks this was given as a very liquid consistency. They were not fed at night.

For the first two or three feeds the chicks may have to be persuaded to open their mouths, but when they are used to the procedure they gape readily at the sight of the feeding implement. Their crops should not be filled to capacity. Chicks never know when they have had enough, and their demands for more food should be ignored. Until they reach the age at which fledging would occur, i.e. about three weeks, they will need to be fed every one to two hours during the day; thereafter, as they start to pick up food, the frequency should be extended until they are feeding quite well on their own, then given a late night feed only as they become independent. As with all chicks, hand-feeding should continue, regardless of age, if they need it, i.e. if they are not taking sufficient food on their own to be well nourished.

Soaked seed, not hard seed, should be offered during the weaning period. The seed should be soaked in cold water for 24 hours, then rinsed under running cold water in a colander before being fed. It is advisable to continue feeding soaked seed until the young are through their first moult, which is the most testing period with finches.

A British aviculturist with very extensive experience of hand-rearing European birds is Frank Meaden. It is unlikely that anyone has hand-fed more European species. The diet he uses for seedeaters is an insectivorous mixture made into a paste with milk. To this is added a pinch of grated cuttlefish bone or calcium lactate, cut-up mealworms and chopped greenfood – either dandelion, comfrey or brassica. Two spoonfuls of the basic mixture are used with twelve mealworms and about half as much greenfood as softfood. Milk is added to give a creamy consistency if the chicks are very young or a crumbly wet consistency if they are over five days old. He recommends feeding mealworms on carrot, apple and celery or high-protein foods, so that some of these are ingested by the chicks.

When they progress to the stage of trying to grab the food being offered, they should be provided with a shallow dish of the rearing food, sprinkled with a little maw seed. Another container, holding red rape, teazle and, for species other than Bullfinches, Chaffinches and Bramblings, hemp seed, should also be available. For these three species, cut-up mealworms should be given instead of hemp. After a week the normal seed mixture, which has been soaked, is offered. This diet is continued, plus the rearing food, until the young have moulted. Small amounts of the leaves of dandelion, comfrey or any brassica are also available.

## SOFTBILLS

The food used by Frank Meaden for hand-rearing softbills does not differ greatly. As a base he uses a high-protein softfood or baby cereal. To two teaspoonfuls he adds twelve chopped mealworms, a pinch of grated cuttlefish bone or calcium lactate and a little finely-chopped dandelion, comfrey or spinach. One drop of Abdec (multivitamins) (Parke-Davis, Pontypool, Monmouthshire, NP4 8YH, UK and Detroit, Michigan, 43232, USA) and a little milk is added to produce a creamy consistency. The food is offered on a spatula.

When the chicks are six days old, grated Cheddar cheese is added, prepared with a fine grater or by pushing it through a metal tea strainer. To start with the cheese forms about 25 per cent of the food and is increased to about one third within a week. As the chicks grow, they are offered, with a tweezer, wax moth larvae, between feeds. First of all the larvae skins should be burst or their heads squeezed with tweezers. (Wax moth cultures can be obtained from specialists in breeding livefood.)

Young softbills should be caged when they peck at the food offered on the spatula. Baby cereal can be discontinued from the diet. They will soon learn to take food from a shallow dish. This should be larger than a saucer and sprinkled with a crumbly mixture of the rearing food, to which grated cheese and cut up mealworms have been added. Frank Meaden describes his method of encouraging young softbills to peck at food as follows.

Ten to twelve maggots are placed under an upturned glass in the centre of the dish. The young bird's attention is drawn to their movements and as it tries to peck at the insects under the glass its beak slips and comes into contact with the rearing food.

As the young start to feed on their own the quantity of moth larvae should be increased and that of mealworms decreased. Abdec should be given in the drinking water twice weekly. After the young have moulted they can be placed in a small outdoor aviary (Meaden, 1979).

The diet for the larger softbills kept by breeders of exotic birds is, of course, rather different. It will vary according to the species and their diet in captivity. As an example, Yellow-billed Hornbills (*Tockus flavirostris*) were hand-reared on crickets (also available from biological and livefood suppliers), mealworms, hard-boiled egg, Mynah pellets, soaked dog kibble, cooked carrots, grapes and meat.

Rare large softbills are occasionally reared by hand. Successes which have occurred in zoos in the USA include Picathartes and a Cock of the Rock, the latter being the first successful breeding in captivity.

Yellow-headed Rock Fowl, also called Bald Crows or Picathartes (*Picathartes gymnocephalus*), are birds of unusual appearance which nest on rocky cliffs in Africa. At San Antonio Zoo in Texas the adult birds are fed

118

on an insectivorous mixture, a meat and fruit mixture, crickets and mealworms. Young are fed by regurgitation. An egg laid in August 1979 was placed in an incubator because the previous egg had disappeared. It hatched after 26 days in a Roll-X incubator set at 37.5° C (99.5° F), and humidity at 30° C (85° F) (wet bulb). A chick hatched and was hand-reared, the success being repeated in 1981 with two chicks. Approximately six hours after the chicks hatched they were fed minute pieces of cricket entrails. The next feed consisted of one bite of chopped pinkie (new-born) mouse dipped in a vitamin solution. These foods were alternated, the chicks being fed every hour for the first three days. On the fourth day they received chopped mouse and cricket entrails at each feed with a piece of water-soaked dog food. The chicks gained 4 to 7 g daily.

On day 10 the feeding frequency was altered to every hour and a half and the food increased. From day 12 the bodies of crickets (with head, legs and wings removed) were offered and feeding frequency was reduced to every two hours. On day 16 white skinned mealworms were introduced to the diet, as well as insectivorous mixture at the ratio of three parts chopped pinkie mouse to one part insectivorous mixture. The proportion of mouse was gradually decreased, then omitted. At 23 days the young were fed four times daily and from the 30th day three times daily. When they started picking up insectivorous food they were making sufficient weight gains to be fed only twice daily.

Hatching occurred during the winter, so the temperature in the brooder was decreased very gradually as follows: 37° C (98° F) until day 9, 35.5° C (96° F) until day 11, 34.5° C (94° F) until day 14, 33° C (92° F) until day 16, 32° C (90° F) until day 17, 31° C (88° F) until day 19, 29° C (85° F) until day 21, thenceforth 27° C (82° F).

The chicks were reared in a bowl 9 cm (3½ in) in diameter, lined with a piece of burlap. After two or three days sticks were placed inside to aid their grasping development. When they started to stand up in the nest at 23 days they were moved to a wire cage which was brightly lit, in contrast to the subdued lighting of the brooder. During the next four days both chicks went off their food and lost weight. At 28 days one died. Its death could not be explained on morphological grounds and it was believed that the different environment, including the bright light and surrounding wire, was responsible for its death. The surviving chick was moved back to the brooder and started to eat and gain weight. It was subsequently found that young adapt to new surroundings very slowly and that the change from dim to bright lighting must be gradual (Solomon and Mills, 1983).

The breeding of the Scarlet Cock of the Rock (*Rupicola peruviana*), mentioned above, occurred at Houston Zoo in 1979, in the large rainforest exhibit. The first chick hatched died at 28 days, probably due

*Scarlet Cock of the Rock* (Rupicola peruviana) *hand-reared by Houston Zoo's Curator of Birds, R. J. Berry. It was the first Cock of the Rock reared in captivity.*

to a reduction in the supply of anoles (small lizards), which had become a favourite rearing food after crickets and mealworms were refused. The female nested again and chicks hatched on December 25 and 26. They progressed well until the age of three weeks when their weight began to fluctuate. They were therefore removed from the nest on January 15 and taken to the home of the curator of birds, R. J. Berry, where they received intensive care.

They were fed hourly on marble-sized balls of a commercial bird of prey food, Zu/Preem (Hill's Division Riviana Foods Inc, POB 148, Topeka, KS 66601, USA), mixed with cat chow. Alternate feeds consisted of pieces of avocado and peeled, halved grapes. The skin was not fed as it was not digested and could have caused compaction of the crop. The eldest chick died of a salmonella infection at 25 days old, which injections had failed to control. The survivor was successfully reared, the diet gradually being changed to consist mainly of cat chow, chopped pink mice and blueberries (grapes appeared not to be suitable). At 46 days it started to pick up and eat pieces of cat chow (small pieces of biscuit). Three days later it left the bowl in which it was kept and made a short horizontal flight (Low, 1980).


## BIRDS OF PREY

Artificial incubation and rearing of birds of prey is much more advanced than that for other non-domesticated birds. This is partly because it has been carried out on a large scale by the Department of Ornithology at Cornell University in the USA, and at other scientific institutions. Carefully recorded results have been made known in many published papers. An especially good source of information on the subject is the *1983 International Zoo Yearbook* (published by the Zoological Society of London) which contains a special section on Birds of Prey. All those interested in artificial incubation and hand-rearing are recommended to read it, as much of the information is applicable to parrots and other species.

A leading raptor breeder in the UK, Robin Haigh (1984) recommends an incubation temperature of 37.2° C (99° F) and relative humidity of 40–45 per cent. At pipping chicks are transferred to a second incubator set at 36.7° C (98° F) and 75 per cent relative humidity. Pip to hatch times are usually 36 to 48 hours but may be up to 75 hours. The temperature in the brooder varies from 36.7° C (98° F) at one end to 34.2° C (94° F) at the other end to provide chicks with a choice of temperature. A 40W red bulb is adequate to give a temperature of 37° C (98° F) directly below the light.

An uneven surface helps to prevent the common problem of splayed legs; crumpled newspaper is covered by towelling, the latter being changed daily. Chicks are kept in cardboard boxes which are replaced about every three days.

Feeding usually commences 12 hours after hatching with one piece of lean meat from the leg of a day-old poultry chick, dipped in cooled boiled water. For a Kestrel a piece the size of half a match head is adequate. Two or three pieces may be given at the second feed; the next day the quantity is increased to four or five pieces per feed. Chicks are fed four times daily. On the third day, liquidised poultry chicks with head, feet and half the yolk sac removed, are offered. On the fourth day a quarter of a teaspoonful of SA37 vitamin and mineral additive (Intervet Laboratories Ltd, Viking Way, Bar Hill, Cambridge, UK) and ⅛ teaspoonful of finest sterilised bone flour are added. After day 12 a small amount of fur is included in the diet. By four weeks the young are given whole liquidised poultry chicks, before being weaned on to small pieces of meat and eventually whole chicks.

A calcium additive such as sterilised bone flour is of vital importance for the young of birds of prey. Without it, and the Vitamin D necessary to allow absorption, rickets are likely to result. Fentzloff (1984) suggested that the extremely marked salivation by the adults while rearing young may indicate that calcium and enzymes are transferred in the saliva. Birds hand-reared on the same food given to parent-reared chicks, but without additives, showed signs of rickets. In the Eagle Owl (*Bubo bubo*) there is a noticeable increase in the calcium content of the saliva of both sexes at the time the young hatch. However, exceeding the calcium requirements will result in the development of brittle bones.

At the German Raptor Centre at Guttenberg Castle, where hundreds of raptors have been reared, symptoms of nutrient deficiency are unknown since using the enzyme solution Enzynorm (Nordmark-Werke GmBH, Hamburg, Uetersen, West Germany). (A pancreatic enzyme available in the UK is Tryplase, Intervet Laboratories Ltd, Science Park, Milton Road, Cambridge CB4 4BH, and in the USA, Entozyme). Pieces of meat to be fed were immersed in one pellet of Enzynorm dissolved in 130 ml of lukewarm water. At London Zoo, Andean Condors have been reared using Tryplase. One capsule was added to 90 g of meat with 50 ml of water. This was incubated at 37° C (98° F) for two hours. The amount of enzyme added to the food is gradually reduced after the Condors are 90 days old (Samour *et al.*, 1984).

In a single decade gigantic strides have been made in the artificial incubation and rearing of raptors, so much that the techniques developed have become a major force in the conservation of a number of species. For example, the Peregrine Falcon is being reared in hundreds for release in the USA (to boost the population which was nearly decimated as the result of the use of DDT). The Mauritius Kestrel (*Falco punctatus*), the rarest falcon in the world, had a wild population of fewer than 15 in 1983, plus six in captivity, three of which had been hand-reared. Since then, hand-rearing has further increased the captive population.

**Food intake and body weight of two Andean Condor *(Vultur gryphus)* chicks hatched at London Zoo (Samour *et al.*, 1984)**

| Days | Food consumed per day (g) | | No of feeds per day | | Body weight (g) | |
|------|--------|------|--------|------|--------|------|
|      | *Female* | *Male* | *Female* | *Male* | *Female* | *Male* |
| 1 | none | none | — | — | 182 | 202 |
| 2 | 14 | 11 | 4 | 3 | 179 | 202 |
| 3 | 17 | 19 | 4 | 4 | 183 | 197 |
| 4 | 31 | 27 | 5 | 4 | 199 | 199 |
| 5 | 43 | 44 | 5 | 4 | 226 | 206 |
| 6 | 46 | 51 | 5 | 4 | 250 | 222 |
| 7 | 48 | 63 | 4 | 4 | 265 | 244 |
| 8 | 70 | 78 | 4 | 4 | 284 | 269 |
| 9 | 157 | 83 | 5 | 4 | 328 | 301 |
| 10 | 108 | 98 | 4 | 4 | 387 | 330 |
| 11–20 | 144 | 164 | 3 | 3 | 686 | 545 |
| 21–30 | 270 | 339 | 3 | 3 | 1,239 | 1,331 |
| 31–40 | 442 | 374 | 3 | 2 | 2,297 | 2,438 |
| 41–50 | 558 | 458 | 3 | 2 | 3,387 | 3,531 |
| 51–60 | 505 | 559 | 2 | 2 | 4,479 | 4,560 |
| 61–70 | 555 | 605 | 2 | 2 | 5,505 | 5,450 |
| 71–80 | 457 | 660 | 2 | 2 | 5,933 | 6,400 |
| 81–90 | 815 | 680 | 3 | 2 | 7,150 | 7,550 |
| 91–100 | 555 | 705 | 3 | 2 | 7,700 | 8,325 |

NB Figures for food consumption and weight from day 11 onwards are averages for the ten-day period.

# BIBLIOGRAPHY

ARMAN, J. and J., 1980, 'Breeding the Yellow-crowned Amazon', *Avicultural Magazine* 86(4): 211–7.

BYERS, B., 1984, 'Some observations when hand-feeding', *San Diego Bird Breeders' Journal* 6(8): 9–15.

CLARKE, P., 1982, 'Breeding the Spectacled (White-fronted) Amazon Parrot', *Avicultural Magazine* 88: 71–4.

COOKE, D., 1985, 'Home-made brooders can save orphans', *Cage and Aviary Birds*, September 7, 1.

COOKE, D. and F., *Keeping and Breeding Cockatiels*, Blandford Press, 1987.

COOPER, N. D., 1968, 'Hand-rearing Golden Mantled Rosellas from the age of one day', *Magazine of the Parrot Society* II(11): 221–7.

COUTTS, G. S., 1981, *Poultry Diseases Under Modern Management*, Saiga Publishing, Hindhead.

EASTMAN, A., 1982, 'Hand-rearing seedeaters', *Cage and Aviary Birds*, August 28, 1.

EMSLIE, J., 1985, 'Breeding Bichenos', *Cage and Aviary Birds*, March 30, 5.

FENTZLOFF, C., 1984, 'Breeding, artifical incubation and release of white-tailed sea eagles', in *1983 International Zoo Year Book* (ed P. J. S. Olney): 18–35, Zoological Society of London.

GRAU, C. R., and T. E. ROUDYBUSH, 1985/6, 'Lysine requirements of Cockatiel Chicks', *AFA Watchbird* 12(6): 12–14.

HAIGH, R., 1984, 'The breeding and artificial incubation of hawks, buzzards and falcons', in *1983 International Zoo Year Book* (ed P. J. S. Olney): 51–8, Zoological Society of London.

HARRIS, R., 1984, 'A first venture with Cockatoos', *Cage and Aviary Birds*, March 24: 1–2.

LOW, R., 1977, 'Hand-rearing Meyer's and Iris Lorikeets', *Avicultural Magazine* 83(1): 12–17.

1980a, 'Breeding the Scarlet Cock of the Rock at Houston Zoo', *Avicultural Magazine* 86(1): 1–4.

1980b, 'Breeding Goffin's Cockatoo', *Avicultural Magazine* 86(4): 195–201.

1982a, 'Hand-rearing Grey Parrots', *Cage and Aviary Birds*, January 9: 3 and 6.

1982b, 'Rearing a Timor Cockatoo', *Cage and Aviary Birds*, March 20: 5.

1983a, 'The Yellow-shouldered Amazon, *Amazona barbadensis*', *Avicultural Magazine* 89(1): 9–20.

1983b, 'First UK breedings of Duivenbode's Lory', *Cage and Aviary Birds*, November 12: 5–6.

1984, 'Breeding Duivenbode's Lory', *Avicultural Magazine* 90(1): 18–26.

1985, 'Breeding the Tahiti Blue Lory', *Avicultural Magazine* 91(1–2): 1–14.

1986, *Parrots, Their Care and Breeding* (second edition), Blandford Press, Poole, UK.

MEADEN, F., 1979, *A Manual of European Bird Keeping*, Blandford Press, Poole, UK.

MERVYN, L., 1984, *The Vitamins Explained Simply*, Science of Life Books, Victoria, Australia.

NOEGEL, R., 1982, 'Life Fellowship breeds Hyacinth Macaws', *Magazine of the Parrot Society* 16(2): 37–40.

1985, 'Captive breeding Hyacinth Macaw', *Magazine of the Parrot Society* 19(39): 77–81.

SAMOUR, H. J., P. J. S. OLNEY, D. HERBERT, F. SMITH, J. WHITE and D. WOOD, 1984, 'Breeding and hand-rearing the Andean Condor at London Zoo', in *1983 International Zoo Year Book* (ed P. J. S. Olney): 7–11, Zoological Society of London.

SMITH, G. A., 1985a, 'The Palm Cockatoo', *Magazine of the Parrot Society* 19(2): 32–40.

1985b, 'Problems encountered in hand-rearing Parrots', *Magazine of the Parrot Society* 19(7): 162–171.

SOLOMON, J. and H. MILLS, 1983, 'Hand-rearing Bald Crows', *The AFA Watchbird* 10(4): 18–21.

# INDEX